BEATING DEPRESSION

BEATING
DEPRESSION

Inspirational Stories of
Hope and Recovery

ROBINSON

Constable & Robinson Ltd
55–56 Russell Square
London WC1B 4HP
www.constablerobinson.com

First published in the UK by Robinson,
an imprint of Constable & Robinson Ltd, 2011

A copy of the British Library Cataloguing in
Publication data is available from the British Library

Important Note
This book is not intended as a substitute for medical advice or treatment.
Any person with a condition requiring medical attention should consult a
qualified medical practitioner or suitable therapist.

ISBN: 978-1-84901-402-1

Typeset by TW Typesetting, Plymouth, Devon

Printed and bound in the EU

1 3 5 7 9 10 8 6 4 2

With thanks to those who have generously and courageously shared their experiences in this book.

Table of contents

Introduction: Personal tragedies and triumphs in the battles with depression

Depression haunts the lives of many millions of people throughout the world. Some estimates put the number at well over 350 million people suffering depression at any one time. This may actually be an underestimate. The World Health Organization suggests that depression will be the second most burdensome disorder in the world by 2020, and for women aged between fifteen and forty-five it's already the most common and debilitating of disorders. In addition, while many of us might not reach the full monty of depressive symptoms we can have many depression-related symptoms that interfere with our lives, confidence and sense of well-being. In fact, depression is something that we can all experience to a lesser or greater degree at some time in our lives. Scientists also know that animals too can behave and look as if they are depressed. This is important because it tells us that a depressed state of mind can occur in many living things and, as we will talk about shortly, this can give us clues about the depressed mind.

In these inspirational stories eight people share their journeys into and out of depression. You will read how they fell into depression, became caught in it, and then how they began to find ways to emerge from it. By reading other people's stories we come to recognize that depression is not 'one thing'. In many ways each person's depression is unique because each of us has a particular set of genes which vary slightly from one another and we have different life experiences that shape us in all kinds of ways, too. In fact, much of the way we have become the people we are was outside our control. For example, I often say to my clients that if I had been swapped as a baby and brought up in a Mexican drug gang the chances are I would either be dead or have killed people myself and be in jail – or possibly be very rich! There is no way at all that this version of me – this Paul Gilbert who has been lucky enough to study in a relatively free Western world and become a psychologist, writing this chapter – would exist. This Paul Gilbert is just one version of many possible versions, but I actually did not have that much choice over which one would become possible. It's the same for all of us. If we think about it, we did not choose our genes: they came from our parents. We did not choose the kind of brain that we have. Our brains have been shaped by evolution and we, like many other animals, are set up to want certain things such as good food, a sense of safety, and being valued and wanted by others. Also we, like other animals, have certain basic emotions designed by evolution and built by our genes. We can become anxious when threatened, angry when thwarted and submissive when in conflict with those more powerful than ourselves. Our background shapes our brain, the values that we endorse and the things we believe about ourselves and others.

Once we understand this we can stand back from our depressions and recognize that blaming ourselves for depression doesn't make any sense. Depression is nothing to do with character weakness or failing or any of those things. Depression affects the rich and poor, the bright and the less intelligent, the kind and the selfish, the old and the young. Depression occurs because our brains switch into a particular pattern. As we will see there are many reasons that can cause it to do that.

In fact, in 1978 I suffered my own depression that was linked to various early life experiences and triggered by a set of complex, and unexpected combination of events. It began with anxiety in unusual (for me) situations – especially those associated with being trapped, such as in shops, queues or at dinner parties. It was soon marked by problems sleeping, seeing life as pointless, hidden rage and with various suicidal ideas. However, luckily for me I had studied depression as a research psychologist and was able to see that our brains are capable of generating all kinds of patterns like this. When we are happy, anxious, hungry, contented, in love, in mourning, or impulsive – these all reflect patterns in our brain (which could be called 'brain states' or 'states of mind'). Depression *is a pattern in our brain* that emerges for many, many reasons. However, depression is not the real me or you: it is a pattern or state that can emerge in us, because we are creatures *of multiple states* and complexions. Evolution built us that way, built us so that we are not 'one club golfers'.

So we are capable of great cruelty and great compassion, quiet confidence and paralysing fear, empathic forgiveness and vengeful anger, reflective thoughtfulness and impulsive thoughtlessness. Sometimes we can even try to define different types of personality within us; the perfectionist, the worrier, the avenger, the critic, the artist, the angry demanding child and so on. We recognize that we can move in and out of these personality-like states of mind. So we need to first think of depression as a brain pattern, a state that is operating through oneself, but is not oneself. After all, water can carry a medicine or poison but water is not the medicine or poison. So taken was I by this view that my first book in 1984 was called *Depression: From Psychology to Brain State*. I wanted to explore how our own psychology, our own ways of thinking and the life events we encounter can affect us by changing patterns in our brains and can trigger all kinds of depressed patterns in us. This helped me keep my depression slightly at arm's length.

The nature of depression

Given these preliminary thoughts, my role in this opening chapter is to offer an overview, a road map if you like, of depression so that you can use it to explore the personal stories offered here. Now, I have already mentioned that depression has many different textures and experiences to it, but even so there is a range of symptoms that typically go with being depressed. Firstly, people lose their motivation to do things, which is partly because they feel very tired a lot of the time. Rather than looking forward to things we often have a feeling of dread. Our emotions change, too. Positive emotions such as enjoying and savouring good things such as a film, meal or a party seem to disappear or get toned down, whereas more unpleasant emotions such as anxiety and anger or irritability increase.

There are changes in how we think, too, when we are depressed. We tend to look at the negative side of things and block out the positives. Actually, you don't need to be depressed to do that because this is how our brains naturally work. Imagine, for example, you go Christmas shopping and nine shopping assistants are very helpful to you and help you buy a present that's better quality for the same price as you were going to buy. You come out of the shop feeling quite pleased. However, supposing one shop assistant is rude to you, they clearly are not interested in trying to help you and because you are a little unsure about what present you want they make you feel foolish . . . and then they short change you! So who are you going to talk about when you go home, who are you going to ruminate about? Are you going to focus on the 90 per cent of people who were really helpful to you? Unlikely. So here's the first problem: through no fault of our own, evolution has designed our minds and shaped them to focus on threats. Over millions of years ago, if animals were enjoying a lovely lunch of fruits or grasses in the savannah and a lion appeared they would have to lose all interest in their tasty lunch, become anxious and focus all their attention on the lion. This makes good sense, of course, because focusing on the possible threat could save their lives. So threat-based emotions, such as anger and anxiety, are designed to be easily aroused and to override and even suppress positive emotions. This happens in so many areas of life, doesn't it? We have an argument with someone we care about and when in an angry state of mind we tend to forget the good side of that person, at least for a while. We will come back to the importance of thinking shortly.

Along with changes in motivation, emotions and ways of thinking, depression brings about changes in behaviour. Partly because we may feel tired or anxious we stop doing things that normally we would either enjoy doing or be able to do. This is called avoidance. When people get into this mode of avoidance problems start to build up for them because they're not tackling them straightaway. As problems build they feel more stressed and want to run away, and so become more avoidant. Similarly, people stop doing things that would normally bring them pleasure. The confident person who enjoys parties may start to avoid them as they become depressed. Research suggests that this 'shutting down' behaviour and avoidance in dealing with one's stresses, and also doing less positive things, contributes to depression. Indeed, one treatment for depression focuses on helping people break problems down, tackle them, find solutions to them and also to engage in positive activities more. Exercise, too, has been shown to be very helpful for some depressed people and becoming inactive in itself can be a source of lowered levels of positive emotion.

Brain systems and depression

Everyone agrees that changes take place in the brain when depression occurs. The debates are on how and why they occur and, of course, how to reverse them. Recent research has enabled us to think about different types of changes related to different types of feelings. It turns out that we have at least three types of 'emotion regulation systems' – the things that control our moods. First, we have emotion systems that evolved to help us detect and deal with threat. There is a key area in our brain called the amygdala which is specifically focused on threat detection and can become very sensitive in depression. Threat emotions, such as anger, anxiety and disgust are heightened, and when we feel depressed we can certainly notice increases in feelings of frustration, irritation and anger as well as apprehension and anxiety. In other words, the threat system is toned up and easily activated.

We also have two types of positive emotion systems. One is linked to our drives and feelings of excitement. For example, if you won the lottery (when not depressed) you would find your body becoming energized, restless, racing from one thing to another, and you would find it very difficult to sleep for the first few days. Actually, you would have a mild hypomania. This is linked to a chemical in the brain called dopamine. Now there are many types of what we call dopamine receptors and there are different areas of the brain in which dopamine is important. Interestingly, people in the pre-depressive period can experience increased drive, racing around and trying to achieve many things. In these stories you will read about people's striving, competing and efforts to achieve more and more. The problem is that these efforts can put our drive system literally into overdrive, running the risk of exhaustion followed by feelings of defeat and inferiority. We know, for example, that when animals are defeated or are stressed to the point they are unable to control the stress they show changes in dopamine levels.

Researchers have also pointed to the fact that our Western societies are increasingly over-stimulating the drive system. Everything seems to be based on having to be excited, from the computer games for our children through to our television programmes. In our schools and work environments there is considerable increase in competitiveness, with fears of failing. It is interesting when you look at many recent programmes on TV, such as *Big Brother*, *The X Factor* and even cooking competitions, it is clear that there has been a change of focus in the last thirty years. Before, competitions would focus on the winners and there would be many losers to hug each other and commiserate. Now each programme focuses on the losers, watching them tearfully leave the competition. Usually losers are dispatched one at a time. The whole focus is on who we are going to throw out this week. So our whole society is increasingly anxious about being good enough, acceptable or unrejectable, and this has effects on our drive system. You will see this theme time and again in the stories that you read – the struggling and striving to prove oneself, to make oneself better, more acceptable, more attractive, more competent and indispensable and to avoid rejection. The level of insecurity and threat for us when we do this is clear. The problem is that depression will become the uninvited guest at the door the moment we start to fail and feel that we can't do it – then we feel, of course, that there is no place for us, that we can't fit in.

The third emotion regulation system is associated with different chemicals in our brain, in particular endorphins and a hormone called oxytocin. We all have had the experience of feeling content and enjoying things in the present moment, of being at peace with ourselves. We have a sense of well-being where we are. This sense of peaceful, contented well-being arises in situations where we feel safe, when we're not struggling with avoiding threats or striving. Importantly, feeling safe is often related to how socially connected we feel. If you look at how young children relate to their parents you will see that when they are threatened they turn to their parents who pick them up, perhaps give them a hug and assure them of being loved. When we are threatened as adults we also like to be able to turn to others for support and care. The more socially connected and supported we feel the less likely we are to become depressed and the quicker we are able to pull out of it if we do.

This third emotion regulation system, then, is key to regulating the other two. One of the reasons we get into overdrive is because we don't feel safe as we are: we feel we have to do extra, be more in control, more perfect and so on. Diagram 1, below, gives an overview of these systems. Depression is basically where we experience the threat system as toned up, whereas our drive and motivational systems – the feelings of looking forward to becoming excited and enjoying things – take a dive and are toned down. We feel exhausted and defeated. However, the second positive emotional system that gives rise to feelings of contentment and social-connectedness also gets toned down. This can leave us feeling socially

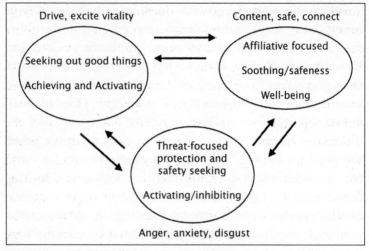

Diagram 1: Types of affect regulation systems

Source: Gilbert, P. (2009) The Compassionate Mind, *with kind permission from Constable & Robinson*

isolated, emotionally cut off from others, not part of things, and struggling to feel cared about or cared for.

So this is what we mean by a depressed brain state: there are specific changes in our emotions and in our motivations, changes in the way we think about things (ourselves, others and the world in general) and changes in our behaviours. All these come with a whole range of changes in the processes in our bodies and brains.

How our brain states can become disturbed

Now for many years scientists have studied how it is that the brain can go into such distressing states, which, on the surface at least, seem unhelpful and useless to our survival. After all, depression doesn't really seem to have much going for it and one might have thought that these states of mind would have been gradually weeded out by evolution. The problem is that evolution doesn't work that way. For example, we know that diarrhoea and vomiting are extremely helpful in getting rid of noxious substances that could harm us. We have evolved the defensive ability to have diarrhoea and to vomit when we need to. Indeed, nowadays doctors may recommend that you don't try to stop your diarrhoea and vomiting for at least forty-eight hours because you want to get rid of the 'bugs' that might be causing the illness. The problem is, though, that this defence can become uncontrolled and people can die, not from the disease, but from the effects of dehydration caused by diarrhoea and vomiting. Diarrhoea and vomiting, which are the body's natural defences, are sadly also big killers of children, especially in developing countries. So why would evolution give us a potential cure that can also kill us? It is all to do with regulation. On the whole it's useful for us to have a body that can defend itself by using diarrhoea and vomiting even though some individuals will die when it becomes long term. Most people will be saved by this defence because it comes on for a short time and then gradually we recover and it stops.

So depression can be understood in a similar way. We are biologically set up to be able to tone down positive emotions and tone up negative emotions in certain contexts. We all acknowledge that anxiety can be useful when we are facing threats. A little anxiety may push us to studying for exams, to be cautious about taking certain risks, but what about toning down positive emotions? What is the value of toning down our ability to feel excited about things or to feel socially connected?

Depression seems to be associated with two types of situation: one is feeling that we have failed in the competitions of life; we might feel inferior or unable to defend against others who are bullying and more powerful. A second situation (which can be linked to the first) is feeling disconnected from sources of care, kindness and being valued. Let's look more closely at the first one. As we have noted, in animals and humans, being subjected to repeated stresses that seem difficult, if not impossible, to control or avoid has major impacts on our brains, and therefore moods. It seems like our brains are designed to shut down when we get overloaded, especially by stresses that seem out of control. In the wild, the most typical repeated stressors with which individuals will be confronted are other animals who are powerful and dominant. This is especially true for individuals who live in groups. Hence, we find that the animals who have been defeated or who are harassed by other animals show depressed-like patterns. If you think about it, it makes sense that animals who are defeated and are being harassed shouldn't be too confident or strut around the place because that is going to increase their risk of being attacked again. Trying to keep a low profile may be the best way to try and protect oneself, even if one feels very angry and wants revenge. So we know that social undermining, criticism, bullying and harassment, which can be mild but constant, are all linked to depression, in both humans and animals.

This is why it's so important that schools and workplaces have very strong anti-bullying policies. Unfortunately we can also experience bullying in our own homes, perhaps from our partners or our parents. There is now considerable evidence that people growing up in households where there is a lot of criticism, and/or low affection, are much more vulnerable to depression than those who grow up feeling secure, loved and valued, with low levels of hostility. Also, of course, it's not just in the home. School bullying is also known to link to depression in children and adolescents. So the effects of being bullied in early life can have long-lasting effects. Many of the people who have written the stories in this book talk to us about the feelings of being bullied and criticized or growing up in families where there was a lot of hostility. It's very difficult to develop a sense of yourself as competent, desired and accepted if you are being criticized all the time.

However, one of the most important sources of bullying in depression is not other people but *ourselves*. Because we are frightened of not being acceptable, or feel inferior in some way, we seek to drive ourselves on. The problem is that when we struggle we start to feel threatened and when we feel threatened we can become frustrated and angry, and this frustration and anger can be directed towards ourselves – 'Why did I do that? Why did I say that? Why couldn't I have been more careful? Why couldn't I have achieved this or that? Why don't I slim down?' It is our own self-criticism that, day in, day out, undermines our sense of confidence and also constantly stimulates our negative emotions. We tell ourselves that we are not good enough, we should not have made this mistake or said that, felt this or fantasized that. We see some of our struggles as evidence of little willpower, or another example of being too fat, unattractive, stupid – the list goes on. Key here are the emotions we direct at ourselves – commonly anger and contempt. When you are next feeling self-critical, take a moment and note *the emotions* in the criticism – then ask yourself – does that self-criticism really have your best interests at heart? So deep inside of ourselves we have this constant undermining system because we haven't learned how to value ourselves as *human beings*. Perhaps one of the most important lessons depression teaches us is that we can become our own worst enemies. As one of my clients once said, 'It was my own self-condemnation that condemned me to depression.'

Typically, animals who have been defeated or who are being harassed live in groups. So they can't get away from the harassment – they are trapped. You won't be surprised to learn that feelings of lacking control and feelings of being trapped are also very common when we become depressed. Indeed, sometimes it's that feeling of entrapment that can lead quite naturally to suicidal thoughts – it's the only way we can see to get out of what is a horrible state of mind or situation. Do keep in mind, though, that this experience of entrapment is common to many depressions and it is not your fault. It's vital that should you start to experience these thoughts you seek help from your GP because these thoughts are part of the depression and the depression can be treated.

We can also feel trapped because we find it difficult to

be honest about our feelings. Maybe we are very angry but are frightened to express it, or maybe we want to leave a relationship but are frightened to be alone or feel guilty about the children, or maybe we think we should put up with a difficult relationship and not be so selfish. Sometimes we know that our anger is out of proportion to the situation and that makes it difficult to express it. Indeed, it is not uncommon to find that some depressed people really struggle with being assertive, and learning assertiveness can be really very helpful for them.

Defeat, setbacks and failures are also common reasons for experiencing low mood. We see this all the time, don't we? For example, imagine you are hoping to pass an exam or you are taking part in an important tennis competition. What will happen to your mood if you pass or win and what will happen to your mood if you fail or lose? Now, the importance of the exam or the competition may well influence the degree of your mood change but it's pretty clear you can feel more positively if you win than if you lose. This is natural. However, there is another aspect of this. Supposing you fail your driving test and you discover that everybody else passed the first time, how do you feel? Now imagine that you learn that no one passes the test first time? All your friends tell you how they felt when they failed too and so you know you're just like them. How do you feel? It turns out that even failures, defeats and setbacks are easier for us to deal with if we feel *we are like others*. However, if we feel that we are somehow inadequate or inferior to others, or that those others are much better than us, then defeats, setbacks and failures become much more depressing.

These thoughts are important because they show that it's easier to deal with defeats and setbacks in the context of feeling socially supported; and it's when we feel that the defeats and setbacks will lead to us being rejected or feeling inferior that there is a problem. The reason for this is that the affiliative and soothing system can play a very major role in how we deal with life difficulties. Indeed, we know that one of the major triggers of depression can be losses, especially of important relationships, or feeling cut off from sources of support, care and affection. This is true for animals, too. Studies have shown that if you separate infants from their parents they showed depression-like patterns of searching for the parent, with pining behaviours, and then if they can't find the parent, they shut down and become quiet, which is sometimes called a 'despair state'. This makes sense because in the wild an infant that is disconnected from its parent would soon attract predators and run the risk of becoming dehydrated in the heat or lost. So a better solution for survival is to turn off positive emotion and any desires to explore and engage the world, and instead hunker down and hope others come to find you. This is like going to the back of the cave, hiding and waiting for better times. Now, if you think about it, and you have had any experience of depression, you know exactly what this feels like. There is the sense of disconnection, of having lost or perhaps never really feeling a sense of connection, and yet there is also the feeling of really wanting someone to come and rescue you, to reach in and somehow connect to you. It is so easy for us to experience these feelings as though they are deeply part of us and to not realize that actually they are part of the way *we are built*. They happen in many individuals, even animals too. So we can stand back from the feelings and start to work with these states of our mind. We can stand back from depression and understand it as something that has been triggered in us, as opposed to something that is bad or inadequate about us.

The power of one's own thoughts

So feelings of loss, feeling disconnected from people, feeling that one isn't cared for by others, feeling trapped, feeling defeated, having thoughts about being inadequate and becoming self-critical are all the lifeblood that feeds depression. However, while we might be able to see the things that fuel depression we humans have another problem. This comes from the fact that we are a species that can think, imagine and are able to hold in mind thoughts and images that maintain our depression!

Compared to animals we have the capacity to think, ruminate, plan, anticipate, fantasize, imagine and reflect. Imagine the zebras on the savannahs of Africa. It is very unlikely that they stay up at night worrying about where the lions will be in the morning, or if their infant might wander off and put themselves in danger, or if they will find enough food or water tomorrow. They will simply respond to the world as it presents itself and react in the moment. Humans do that, of course, but we also have a lot going on inside our heads. Humans would think ahead about where lions are likely to be and avoid those areas. By planning ahead and anticipating possible threats we have a brain that can help us survive, but there is a catch to this. This brain can also lead to us ruminating about threats in the future (which we call worry) and harmful things that may have happened to us in the past (rumination). We are a species who tends to turn things over and over in our minds, both looking forwards and backwards in time.

This understanding is incredibly important for working with depression and many of the people in the stories you will read have come to understand this. They have come to understand that what *sits* in their mind – what they ruminate on and what they focus on – plays a major role in their depression and can trap them in their depression. The simple reason for this is that we know that *what* we think about – *how* we ruminate and what images we create in our minds – can have powerful effects on our bodies and our minds. For example, if we are hungry and see a meal, this can stimulate our saliva and stomach acids. Equally, if we just fantasize about a meal, merely imagining the food can also stimulate our saliva and stomach acids. Another good example of how our imagination can stimulate our bodily processes can be seen when we fantasize about somebody to whom we are physically attracted. In this respect *our body responds to our imagination* in a similar way that it responds to the real world.

Similarly, if we are angry and we imagine arguing – you know the kind of thing, going over and over what we might say to them and so on – this will affect our brain and bodily processes. If there are things that we are anxious about and we imagine something frightening happening to us, this will stimulate our anxiety system. On the other hand, if we focus on something we are looking forward to, such as imagining a happy holiday, this will give us a little buzz of excitement. So, imagery then affects our feelings, thoughts and our bodies. The point is: ask yourself what sits in your mind day in, day out. Consider that what is sitting in your mind day in, day out will be affecting your body in major ways, through no fault of your own; it's the way we are made. Even though we have paid the price it's very helpful to be able to stand back and really start thinking about and reflecting on what actually goes through our mind day by day. You see, the thing is that if the threat system becomes over-stimulated it will constantly throw threats at you. Remember we talked about Christmas shopping? Again, it's not your fault that you have become unhappy because of the attitude of one of the shop assistants, but it may not be in your best interest to allow the threat system to have its own way all the time. The threat system is not very bright: it's been designed to respond quickly and protect you, not to think things through carefully or to focus on your feelings of well-being.

Therapy

So this brings us to the issue of therapy and what can help people. You will read many examples of people discovering things for themselves, sometimes with the help of the therapist, sometimes just by coming to an awareness that how they think, what they think about and what they dwell on is the key to helping them stay in or gradually shift out of depression. Many of the people who have written these stories have come to realize that depression is a brain state, a pattern of activity in our brains, and that we can begin to take steps deliberately to change these patterns by refocusing our attention and refocusing on what we think about and how we behave in the world. Like starting to become physically fit, if we are unfit and overweight the first steps are not easy ones. We have to put effort into it and sometimes it's a bit of a struggle, but if we keep our focus and make an effort we will gradually get fit.

Most therapies today teach people to pay particular attention to what is going on in their minds moment by moment, hour by hour, day by day. When people notice that they are being very self-critical, or ruminating on things that make them anxious, or are focusing on feelings of inadequacy, the trick is for them to redirect their attention to more helpful, positive ideas or images. Sometimes people are taught what is called 'mindfulness', where they learn to notice the thoughts and images going through their minds but then not to get caught up in them, to refocus on their breathing perhaps or simply to bring attention to the here and now, to one's senses, to the sky above or the ground below one's feet, or the act of breathing or walking. The point of this is that it stops the mind constantly generating and regenerating negative loops that can feed depression.

Other therapists teach people not to take their thoughts at face value or as facts, but to learn to stand back from immediate reactions to things or typical ruminations and explore if there are alternative ways to think. Remember the Christmas shopper above? What would happen to the person who simply kept ruminating about the rude shop assistant in comparison to the person who recognized the rumination and instead thought, 'Yes, that was a rude assistant but it's important not to get stuck with that and to stand back and think about the whole day and remember that 90 per cent of people were really helpful.' The second person would then bring to mind those interactions, remember the smiling face of a helpful assistant and remember exactly how they felt as they came out of the shop, pleased with the present they had bought, and so on. Think about what will be happening in the brains of these two different people. You can see how important it is to focus on the more positive things: you have to train your mind to do this because your threat system will automatically take control if you let it – it's your factory setting, it's what it's designed to do.

We might feel like failures but that's the way depression thinks and is not the way we think when we are not depressed. Some therapists will help people recognize that there are unprocessed emotions and memories that are haunting them and undermining their sense of confidence, their belief in love, their ability or value. One reason we can feel powerless in the world is because we don't know how to be assertive or how to deal with anger. Maybe anger makes us feel guilty and we keep pushing it away.

In one type of therapy, called Compassion Focused Therapy, people are invited to spend some time imagining themselves at their best, at their most compassionate, as the person they would really like to be. From that position, people can then engage with their distressing feelings or thoughts, but always from a compassionate, authoritative point of view. The point of developing the experience of the compassionate self or imagining a compassionate voice is that we want to stimulate the affiliative system – the system that involves feeling safe and contented – in our brains. It's a deliberate attempt to take control of our brains and minds. Just as going to the gym or for a run is a deliberate attempt to stimulate your body to lose weight and build muscle, so practising certain kinds of imagery and exercise is a deliberate attempt to stimulate your brain in a certain way. There is evidence that if we practise stimulating our brains in a certain way then our brains actually do change.

What all these approaches have in common is that they recognize that depression is a complex mental state but that we can create conditions which make it more likely to heal. This doesn't mean that we ignore outside difficulties such as severe poverty or abusive marriages. Indeed, by becoming more compassionate we sometimes have to become more courageous and face up to the things that we know are the source of some element of our depression. In some of the stories you will read how people began to recognize how they needed to find their own courage to change things in their lives, but when they did so it was very helpful to them in their depression.

Depression can also be a time when we start to close down from the help that is available. We know that depression is steadily increasing in Western societies and this is partly because we're becoming too isolated from each other rather than recognizing that all of us are vulnerable to these painful states of mind to one degree or another. The more we are open with each other, reach out to each other, and accept and give help to each other, the more of a caring society we become and therefore we become less vulnerable to depression. This is why these stories are so important – they are not health professionals but people like you and me who are struggling with painful states of mind and finding a way through.

Physical help

Understanding that depression is a change of brain state means that we should not neglect the physical side and sometimes working on that directly can be helpful. In fact, as our writers in this book show, some of them also benefited from taking medication – while others did not. The evidence here is tricky because studies suggest that the more severe the depression the more helpful an antidepressant could be. Some people find them useful because they help with sleep and take the edge off things. Other people can feel worse on them. It's important to keep in mind, however, that there are different types of antidepressant and research suggests that if you don't benefit from one you could benefit from another. Moreover, some people have worse side-effects on one type than another type. Some antidepressants are more slowing while others make you feel more active. So it's very important to stay in touch with your GP and talk about your experiences of an antidepressant if you are offered one or choose one. You should also keep a note if you experience side-effects from other medications that might link to depression. For example, some recent concerns have been raised about statins (which reduce cholesterol) because of their effect on people's moods and memory. Once again, if you suspect this then talk to your GP.

If you feel physically unwell and extremely tired then, again, a trip to your GP is recommended because some kinds of physical conditions such as diabetes, hyperthyroidism and other conditions can impact on our moods, and it is important to check these out. New research is also beginning to suggest that viruses and other factors that affect our immune system could influence depression. We now know that the immune system and the chemicals in our brain related to moods have very powerful and complex interactions that are only just beginning to be understood.

There is also increasing evidence that our diets may contribute to depression, particularly the processed high-carbohydrate diets we are subjected to today (chips, pies, hamburgers, you know the sort of thing). Traditional diets which involve fruits, vegetables, beef, lamb, fish and wholegrain foods – in other words low-carbohydrate, less-processed foods – are associated with lower depression rates. It's certainly worth trying this type of diet for a week or two just to notice if you feel less bloated, have more energy and feel less depressed. There is also evidence that Omega-3, folic acid and other supplements could be helpful for some people. The key here is getting the right dose. Some people also benefit from exercise because this stimulates endorphins and some people are very sensitive to changes in their endorphins, which can produce a feeling of well-being. People who have seasonal affective disorder (SAD), that is they get depressed during the darker months and tend to experience an increase in sleeping, can benefit from light therapy. So there is a range of physical interventions people can look into for help with depression and it's important to explore what works for you, but always check them out with your GP.

Overview

If you struggle with depression I hope you find that these stories resonate with your experience, but most of all that you see there are ways out of depression and that help is available (please also see the chapter on support groups and other resources at the end of this book). I always remember an old tutor of mine saying that depression is best viewed as a form of exhaustion where we become emotionally, physically and intellectually exhausted. If we learn to recognize this, we can begin to try to rebuild our energies, first of all by being kind, supportive and understanding of ourselves. We can also reach out for help, talk to others about our feelings and check out if there's anything physical that we need to talk about with our general practitioners.

Many of the stories you will read here note how important the help of others was for them – so it is important we do not suffer in silence or in shame. Depression is very common today, with one in four or five of us suffering from it at sometime in our lives. It is time for us all to acknowledge this, reach out and help each other. Depression is a feeling of barriers and isolation – opening up to others can be a way out. So by sharing their journeys into and out of depression these authors hope you will be able to take courage and inspiration to reach out and find people who can help you. Many compassionate wishes to you on your life's journey.

Professor Paul Gilbert

1

Eat more bananas

The woods were silent that day. They were devoid of colour, scent, sound and movement, as they had been for countless days. As I walked amongst the ancient trees, once the hunting grounds of Henry VIII, with my dog Bella by my side, I felt no enjoyment, no inspiration, no peace. Where once I had found pleasure and solace, nothing that morning could enthuse my struggling spirit or calm the turmoil in my head.

I was a thirty-nine year-old woman living life comfortably with a great job, a wonderful family and faithful friends. I was brought up in Sussex and had a blissful childhood, spending most of my time exploring the nearby forest with my older brother. Life was rather good. I worked from home as a freelance photographer and a creative assistant for a businesswoman. Although there was a huge amount of pressure, and I was on call 24/7, it was exciting and I didn't have children or a mortgage, so I focused entirely on my job, which had huge diversity with no day ever being the same.

My favourite declaration was 'I'm fine.' I always avoided talking about myself, or how I was feeling, not wanting to bore others with my problems and thoughts. But underneath the bravado I was a chronic worrier – worrying about my friends and their problems; worrying about deadlines, my weight; upsetting people; and worrying about my family. Basically, I was worrying about worrying and if I had nothing immediate to worry about, I'd find something, however minute, and out would come my mental worry beads. With hindsight, I now know that for years I was running on pure adrenaline: my nerves were stretched as tightly as the strings on a harp, my mind and body permanently on red alert, and I could never sit still. My father had once described me as a firework – noisy, lively and always racing off at a tangent.

I started to try too hard – tried to be the best friend, the indispensable employee, the funniest, the most creative, the brightest, the most cheerful, the most supportive and caring, and, most dangerously, always available, never leaving myself any time just to be still, to breathe, to unwind. I was spreading myself so thinly, it was inevitable that something would have to snap under the intolerable pressure that I heaped upon myself. I was like a runaway train, hurtling along blindly, perilously unaware that, soon, I would run out of track.

I held many fears and anxieties close to my heart: I was scared of flying and driving on a motorway; I didn't like being away from home; I got hideously nervous at parties and meetings, but I concealed my fear by trying to be exuberant, funny and fun. At parties, if a man asked me what I did, I would come out with some baffling, idiotic response saying that I was a bus driver, or a biscuit designer, or (my favourite) a ballet dancer and how relieved I was not to be wearing my tutu. I thought that if

I was funny, I would be liked, but I must have come across as being facetious and flippant. I had an appalling body image, too. I had always felt overweight, especially in the company of my skinny friends, and having red hair, pale skin and freckles certainly made me different. Childhood taunts of 'ginger nut', 'copper knob', 'Duracell' and 'four-eyes' (I also wore ghastly NHS spectacles) haunted me through my childhood and into my teens.

I always wore black or dark colours, trying to conceal my body and not wanting to stand out in a crowd. I also wore heavy makeup – a mask which hid my naturally pale complexion and freckles.

In a rapidly changing world I felt rather insignificant – I hadn't been blessed with children, so had no legacy to leave behind (for whatever reason, my knight in shining armour had clearly taken a wrong turn and never appeared). I still lived with my parents and had never left home for the simple reason that I was happy there. I had no desire to travel, to experiment, to be a social butterfly. But I felt as if I was being left behind.

Having had pretty disastrous relationships in my twenties, I adopted a different stance in my thirties – life was so much easier on my own and I was comfortable in my own space. Many of my friends had been through ugly divorces and I certainly didn't want to put myself at the risk of a broken heart and shattered dreams.

Looking back, I should have seen the signs that the equilibrium in my life was unhinged. There were many days when life became a little too taxing, and my body was taut with nerves, frustration and pent-up emotion. I would wake every morning with a screaming headache and swarms of butterflies in my stomach, having had a restless night due to my brain's inability to disengage. There was the odd day when I felt on the verge of tears, but I put it down to hormones and getting older, and brushed my feelings aside, ignoring their constant pleas for help. I combated this by rushing to the gym or running in the forest, often with a notepad and pen in one hand and my mobile phone in the other.

Each morning I would wander through the woods with Bella, trying to absorb the peace and the fresh air. But inside, my mind was always a maelstrom of antagonistic thoughts; I was never able to switch my brain off or silence the merry-go-round of noise inside my head. I always had a vivid imagination, and often got lost in a world of daydreams, but I was unaware that, for some time, I had been consumed with self-absorption, anticipating the day ahead with trepidation, predicting catastrophes and negative thoughts. Gradually, I had begun to ignore all that was around me. Where once I had marvelled at the first bluebells of spring, the first call of a cuckoo, the autumn colours and the scent of wild honeysuckle on the breeze – all of these simple pleasures now simply vanished as I walked, day after day, head down, with a mind racing towards a mental breakdown.

It was two weeks before Christmas when my mind catastrophically imploded. It was the busiest time of year for me and I woke one Monday with a dreadful feeling of fathomless fear and a constricting knot in my stomach. My nerves were excruciatingly on edge and I felt horribly sick. My morning walk with Bella failed to calm me and, as my mobile phone rang incessantly, feelings of panic began to gallop through my head like wildebeest hurtling across the Serengeti plains. I sat on a fallen tree and tried to take long, deep breaths, but my heart was pounding and the cacophony of noise in my head was relentless. I was tearful, and fearful, and felt that I was about to slide down a treacherous slope into a puddle of tears and there was nothing I could do to stop my fall. These feelings were somewhat alien to me; I wasn't one to cry easily and I had always kept my emotions buttoned up, close to my heart, guarded with my stiff upper lip. I couldn't understand where the tears were coming from and why they constantly pricked my eyes. Throughout that day they were menacingly close. I held it together, just.

As Tuesday dawned the work-pace increased, my lip was permanently quivering and I couldn't help but cry. I was unable to concentrate and found even the simplest of tasks impossible.

My morning walk, which once had been the perfect way to start a day, was ruined as my phone constantly screeched, exacerbating the chaos in my head. Even the gentle footsteps of Bella by my side and the soft December sun failed to keep the dark, gathering storm clouds in my mind at bay.

I staggered through the day, desperately trying to hide the fact that I was rapidly unravelling.

At 6.30 p.m. I fled to my yoga class, with puffy eyes, blotchy skin and feeling as if I was about to explode. I felt shaky, agitated, and my stomach was churning; my head felt the size of a watermelon which was full of dynamite, and my heart felt that it could spontaneously rupture. I couldn't think coherently. It was as if I had an orchestra in my head – all playing their instruments but from different concertos – a dissonance of chaos racing around my brain. I couldn't breathe, my breaths coming in rapid succession as if my lungs were devoid of oxygen.

I tried to force myself to relax in the yoga studio; I frantically fought with my mind, screaming inside my head the words 'breathe' and 'relax'. I looked out of the window, watching the silhouettes of deer grazing in the moonlight. THE PROOFS – oh my God – I had forgotten to send some images through to a client, the deadline having been hours ago. My brain raced and my scant concentration evaporated.

After an hour of mental torture, I was desperate to get home. The class ended and I fled, driving home across the forest at ridiculous speed. I charged through the front door, hurtled up the stairs and began emailing the proofs frantically. I read the email over and over and over again; my mind was rushing towards insanity and I didn't trust myself to get the email right.

Strung out and exhausted, I went downstairs for a large glass of wine and dinner. Still the mobile rang with calls from America until 10.30 p.m. and, of course, trying to be indispensable, I answered them.

I went to bed exhausted, desperate to sink into oblivion and to awake, feeling refreshed. I was dreading the next day, knowing it would bring yet more of the same – and thinking WHY CAN'T I COPE? I usually did, this was nothing new – I had been doing it for years and I thrived on pressure, often working more efficiently than during the quiet times. I felt completely out of control of my mind and body, and I was terrified – what could possibly be happening to me? The more I panicked, the more hysterical I became in my head. I felt as if I was on an endless helter-skelter, going round and round, down and down into an abyss of darkness.

On the Wednesday morning I felt wretched as I walked with Bella and spoke to a work colleague whilst marching through the woods. I couldn't stop crying, the tears coming over me in waves, drenching my soul. Every little thing seemed monumental. Logistics of anything related to work seemed unfathomable – my world was spiralling out of control.

How I got through that day I will never know. I was probably using up the last of my resources, the very last drop of adrenaline, and the final ounce of my strength, yet still I was unable to recognize that my body was screaming for help. I was hanging on, by the skin of my teeth, to the precipice of lucidity.

Thursday, 15 December, was the day I lost my mind. I woke up crying, I ate breakfast crying, I walked with Bella crying, and however hard I tried, I couldn't stop the endless downpour of tears. Everything ached – my head, my body, my back, my stomach. I felt physically sick. I tried to think happy thoughts but my mind couldn't think of anything remotely pleasant. There was only darkness. I wanted to stay in my woods. I dreaded going home. I longed to stay in a place where I felt safe and alone and away from the world. I wanted to run as far away as possible, not stopping until I reached the sea, or the mountains, or the hills.

Eventually, I went home and started to read through my emails but the words were blurred and I just couldn't understand them.

I felt that I was caught up in a whirlpool of emotion and I was unable to keep my head above water; I was drowning inside, being sucked into a bottomless pit of despair. I collapsed in a heap on the floor and sobbed uncontrollably, rocking backwards and forwards. Everything seemed to crash down on top of me, all at once. I couldn't get up. I was in the eye of a force twelve hurricane which was destroying everything in its path, mercilessly decimating every ounce of my being.

It was as if my body didn't belong to me, that I was watching myself from afar, not in touch with my physical being. My chest heaved and my stomach was gripped with spasms, expelling my breath and contracting uncontrollably. I was engulfed in the most constricting mental pain and my mind was racing and falling into a chasm of hopelessness. I was suffocating in my mind – I was unable to think, to breathe, to feel.

Mum heard my muffled anguish and came to my side. She was, at the time, playing downstairs with my four-year-old nephew, who was getting ready to go to his Christmas party, dressed as an engine driver. I could tell by her face that she was shocked to see me in such a wretched state. She had watched my father struggle with two episodes of severe clinical depression and instantly knew the signs.

She administered one of my father's diazepam, one of five different drugs that he takes for his depression, a condition that has haunted him for thirty years, and then she called the health centre, making an appointment for me later that afternoon. I lay on my bed, curled in a ball, sobbing. I was petrified; these emotions and the physical anxiety were so alien to me that I feared for my sanity and felt completely out of control.

Dad came upstairs. My parents had known for some days that I was down, and not myself, but when Dad saw me, he realized the full extent of how I was feeling and wrapped me in his arms, holding me tightly, talking softly. His comfort and embrace calmed me down and my uncontrollable sobbing reduced to a persistent weep. But the tears would not stop, they just kept pouring down my face and I became blind with crying. He kept holding me, trying desperately to ease my pain.

When I was eight, Dad became ill with severe clinical depression and battled the illness for three years. With a young family and a mortgage, he had to carry on working, despite the severity of his illness and unsophisticated, and potentially harmful, antidepressants. In those days, depression was rarely discussed or understood, and Dad was often confronted with unsympathetic attitudes and advice such as 'pull yourself together'. We now know that there is a strong genetic link within our family which indicates depression. After the Second World War my grandfather, who had been missing presumed dead in Burma, was returned home and institutionalized. He was given electroconvulsive therapy twice a week but whether this was for depression or another mental illness we will never know. My cousin and a second cousin have both suffered with severe clinical depression in recent years. If a member of the family has had a major depressive episode then, many scientists believe, relatives will have a genetic predisposition to the illness. Women are also more likely to have depression than men.

Dad became ill again in 2002 and fought his depression for another three years, so when I first became ill, he was the one person who knew about mental torture, understanding exactly what was happening to me, and he tried to reassure me that I would survive this moment of madness.

As Dad hugged me tightly, my nephew came to say goodbye before Mum took him to his party, and, with his dear little face etched with a frown, asked Mum, 'Grannie, why hasn't she got a happy face?' I just looked at him and couldn't speak.

When Mum came home, she phoned my closest work colleague and friend, and told her emphatically that I would be unable to work for some considerable time. My friend was amazing. She took complete control of all of my work and assured me that she would deal with everything. Having Mum swiftly act to unburden me with anything remotely stressful was a colossal relief.

Mum came with me to see the doctor that afternoon and, as I sat in the waiting room, I stared at the door, dreading anyone I knew coming in and seeing me, red-faced and in a state of severe agitation. To my relief, I didn't have to wait long until I was called in by a locum doctor. Once more, the dam burst and Mum had to explain what was happening as I was unable to speak coherently. Sympathetically, the doctor spoke to me in a kind way, telling me that I was showing all of the classic signs of depression. He prescribed a course of escitalopram antidepressants. I felt as if I had been handed a lifejacket that would keep me afloat and stop me from sinking even deeper into the sea of confusion. The enormity of the diagnosis simply didn't register with me. I was so consumed with desperation, that I barely understood a word that the doctor spoke.

Normally, I am one of those people who loathe taking any form of medication. If I have a headache I will try everything before resorting to a painkiller. However, faced with this situation, I was hugely relieved when he handed me the green prescription slip – I knew that I couldn't do this alone and desperately needed help. With the aid of another diazepam, I went to bed, sobbing until the drug kicked in and I fell into a deep and dreamless sleep.

I awoke on Friday morning feeling wretched. I made myself get up and take Bella for her morning amble after taking the first tablet from my prescription. I felt exhausted. I dragged my body through the woods and couldn't wait to get home. Each footstep was an effort and it felt as if I was walking through thick mud in steel boots.

I got home, made some tea and went to lie on my bed. And I slept. And slept. And slept. Looking back, I had obliterated all of my natural resources – especially adrenaline – and I was completely spent. After years of living on my nerves and never stopping, of never having holidays or lazy Sundays, it was no wonder that I was experiencing not only a mental breakdown, but also physical collapse.

Soon, Christmas was upon us but my world was in pieces and the very last thing I wanted to face was frivolity. This season was not the season to be jolly. I didn't feel merry or happy. I didn't want to rejoice, celebrate, laugh or be sociable; I didn't want to eat or drink. I just wanted to hide. Somehow, I managed to struggle through the endless festive days, cleverly masking my inner confusion, and telling friends and family that I was suffering with flu. Only my parents and my three closest friends knew the truth.

I constantly worried about work. I had never had this amount of time off ill and, because I was working freelance, I wasn't paid for any absences; and there was a tax bill to pay by the end of the following month. I knew that I needed to rest, that I had a debilitating illness and couldn't possibly work, but I was also aware that I needed to earn money and was appalled at the thought of letting my clients down. So I was constantly fighting the illness, desperate to be well enough to return to work, trying to summon the strength I once had to keep on going. Little did I know that the illness would rapidly become more severe and I would spend endless months shackled with depression.

After a few days of taking the escitalopram, I expected to feel marginally better, but there was no change in my mood – the feelings of hopelessness were still dominating my mind and, if anything, I felt that I was sinking ever deeper downwards. I now know that antidepressants can take several weeks to work – and, in the meantime, the illness can become more intense and the side-effects more permanent. Whilst taking the escitalopram I suffered from chronic nausea, so much so that I lost half a stone in weight.

The following week I made an appointment to see my

GP who reassured me that the medication would soon begin to take effect and my mood would lift. In many cases, depression, if caught early on, can shift within weeks, which is what we were hoping for. But we hadn't taken into consideration the genetic link. Dad had been ill for three years during both episodes of his depression, so my recovery was more than likely to be as slow.

After another ten days I went back to my GP and, through muffled sobs, told him that the tablets weren't working and I clearly needed something stronger. He took me off the escitalopram and prescribed mirtazapine. He also suggested that I should see a consultant psychiatrist and gave me a recommendation.

Almost as soon as I started to take the mirtazapine, I began to suffer from debilitating side-effects which made me feel physically dreadful. Although the nausea subsided, my joints began to swell up and then became painful; I had mouth ulcers, headaches and suffered from constipation, which became a constant side-effect. And the worst was feeling permanently drowsy. So now my mental illness had, in a sense, become a physical illness, too, as each day was dogged with some symptom or another.

An appointment came through to see the consultant psychiatrist I had been recommended at 7 p.m. on Friday, 20 January, at an independent mental health care facility an hour's drive away. My parents took me there in the driving rain and, during the journey, I was wracked with nervousness and anxiety. I was about to meet a complete stranger, who was highly respected in mental health, and I had to tell him how I felt. What if he thought I was spoofing, that I didn't really have depression, that I really *did* just need to get a grip and pull myself together? How could he see inside my head? And, most importantly, could he cure this malignant sadness?

I entered the clinic and registered with the receptionist. The consultant came to meet me and took me to his consulting room via a labyrinth of corridors and locked doors. I was somewhat perturbed that, here, they locked people in – or out. Surely I wasn't that bad. Or would I be locked up, too? Years ago I would have been labelled a 'lunatic' or an 'imbecile', banished to a Victorian asylum to provide entertainment for the noble classes who would visit the institution for amusement. Or I would have been subjected to a spinning stool and spun around rapidly at a hundred revolutions a minute in the hope that the errant components of my brain would somehow fall back into their correct place. Or I would have been muzzled and purged with leeches. I wondered if that's what the psychiatrist had in his consulting room.

He was a young, compassionate and understanding man, and we talked for an hour. He asked me a mountain of questions regarding my childhood, my relationships, my work, my family, my interests, my feelings and the start of my illness. I tried to explain that I felt like a ball in water, with some force infinitely stronger than me repeatedly pushing me beneath the surface, not letting me float to the top; how I had the theme tune to *Bob the Builder* going round and round in my head incessantly; how I couldn't bear the sound of music or noise, or even birdsong. I had to take off my heavy gold bangles that I always wore, because I couldn't stand the sound of them jangling; nothing or no one could interest me; I didn't want to see my friends or even my family; every time the telephone rang I leapt out of my skin; I was permanently exhausted and couldn't shake off the feeling of absolute sadness that enshrouded my heart. The tears just would not stop, especially at night; tears before bedtime were the worst – I simply couldn't face another day.

The consultant sat and listened to my ramblings as I sniffed and wept and constantly shook my head. He suggested that, as well as medication, I should consider cognitive behavioural therapy (CBT) and recommended a therapist. He concurred with my GP regarding the medication and dosage, and asked me to see him again in two weeks' time.

On leaving, he assured me that he could help me to overcome the illness, but it would take time and medication, along with the therapy. That was all I wanted to hear: for someone to tell me that it wouldn't last forever – it was like a beacon of light in my sad, dark little world.

I would continue to see my psychiatrist regularly over the next four years. With hindsight, I now know that I was incredibly lucky to have been able to see him so quickly, right at the beginning of my illness, and I was also fortunate to be able to afford to see a private consultant. When my father became ill with depression, the second time, he had sought help from a private consultant as the NHS waiting list for a psychiatrist was far too long and he needed immediate help. So when I became ill, my parents didn't hesitate in seeking a leading consultant for me in the hope that the depression would be dealt with quickly. However, nobody was aware that the illness was already entrenched and, in fact, became considerably worse in the months to come. I became even more reclusive and unable to relate to anything or anybody.

Even now, I still see my psychiatrist, although less frequently, but I know that his expertise and guidance is invaluable to me – I think of him as the gatekeeper of my mind.

When you are overcome with depression, you are forced to go to a very strange and ominous place in your mind. It's almost like diving to an unfathomable depth in the ocean, where no one has ever been before and where only you can go. You desperately try to swim to the surface, but the illness keeps dragging you down and just as you seem to be making a little progress, down you go again, only this time you reach a deeper, darker place.

Your entire life is in turmoil. You fear for your sanity and feel that you have completely lost control of everything in your mind and therefore your life. It's as if thick black treacle has invaded your very being, seeping into every cell and reaching the cellars of your soul, suffocating you in darkness.

That is why this illness is so isolating – even when talking to someone else who has suffered with severe depression, with recollections of their own experiences, it becomes clear that no two cases are the same inasmuch as our minds are uniquely different and depression manifests itself mentally in many varied ways. It is a life-altering experience and you are forced to change very quickly. But, having had years of experience of living with depression, the most fundamental fact to cling on to is that you *can* recover fully. Depression is a self-limiting illness (that is, an episode will eventually come to an end in due course) and, if treated correctly, the chances of a recurrence are shortened. I've been told that if you have one episode of severe depression, you have a 50 per cent chance of having another.

When I was in the very depths of my depression it was impossible to believe that I would ever smile again. But I did. Recovery from depression is like learning to walk. You see the world through very different eyes and each tentative step, however slow, sets you in the direction of a new path, a new beginning, and, despite how daunting it may be in those early days, you are going forward in the right direction. There may be days when you feel that you are slipping back, but it is important to remember that you have taken the first steps away from your illness and you are leaving it behind, not taking it with you.

I was desperate to find out more information about clinical depression. I spent hours laboriously trudging through the internet in search of information not only on the illness, but also on the drugs and their side-effects. I longed to read of someone else's account that would relate to my own personal struggle. I found books written by eminent psychiatrists, psychologists and doctors but I thought they were too impersonal, offering only a general overview on how one should feel or what one should do. Some books angered me, some I felt ambivalent about, but not one touched a chord within my tortured soul. I just wished that there was a 'manual' for depression. When you buy a kettle there is a leaflet on what to do if it doesn't work. It's such a shame that there is no such thing for when your brain blows up.

And I couldn't find any information on the side-effects

of the drugs apart from a list of possible symptoms. I wanted to know *why* a serotonin-norepinephrine reuptake inhibitor (SNRI) that I was prescribed caused me chronic constipation. How can an antidepressant cause swelling of the joints or nausea? Having an inquisitive and overactive mind, I always wanted to find the answers to my own questions. But here I drew a blank. If, on the drug's patient information leaflet it explained why the body responds in certain ways, I would have been much more accepting about taking the various antidepressants. My world had disintegrated; I was burdened with a fiendish illness. All I wanted was to feel mentally strong again and it was a monumental effort to keep living. I really didn't need a catalogue of physical problems, too. I was at my lowest ebb and I looked dreadful with a haggard, startled expression, bags upon bags under my eyes and I was putting on weight. How could I be positive and carry on? I knew what Van Gogh meant when he said, 'This sadness will last forever.'

As each day passed in agonizingly slow time I began to feel that I was losing a part of who I once was and I no longer knew what I had become. The worst thing about my illness was knowing that I was not me.

During those endless days, I struggled to find some semblance of normality and cheerfulness – happiness was not within my mental grasp but there were moments, that I called my 'chocolate drops' which gave me hope and a gentle reminder that there was a little sunshine for my soul to bask in. At night, lying in bed, I would wonder at the sound of the owl calling hauntingly into the night sky. My nephew was the one person who could make me smile. We sat and watched endless films from beneath the camp we made from cushions and throws, munching jammy dodgers, chocolate fingers and drinking lemonade. The simplicity of a child's world was all that I could cope with. We would spend hours playing with toy cars or paddling along the streams in the forest, frequently in water-filled squelchy boots. We read books and played trains with saucepan lids for steering wheels; we had picnics and sat on the roots of the largest tree in the forest where we sang silly songs and made up stories. We played hide and seek in the woods, picked blackberries and chestnuts. The simplest of pleasures were found in the simplest pursuits. He has always had a wonderful sense of humour and he taught me how to smile again. Each time he hugged me tight or told me he loved me, my fragile heart would constrict. I could escape into my nephew's world where I felt safe and cherished by a four-year-old boy – my sunbeam.

My parents were incredible. They knew when I needed to be alone or when I needed someone to dry my tears; they fielded phone calls and visits and protected me from the outside world. Each week, Mum would come with me to see my psychiatrist or for my CBT therapy sessions, and she would sit in the car for an hour, waiting until the appointment finished. I could see how anxious my parents were about my mental state and I tried desperately to hide them from my private hell. I had an overwhelming need to be alone and night after night I would write in my diary, 'I crave solitude. I need to be quiet. I need to rest, to heal, to sleep. I feel nothing. I am wretched and worthless and useless.'

Dad was the one person who truly understood the illness, although he had been crippled more with anxiety whereas I was consumed with the depression. In fact, when I became ill, I think that he finally became more accepting of his own illness. He had overcome his anxiety and depression solely with medication, refusing any form of therapy – talking therapies were simply not for him. But when he saw that I was willing to talk openly about depression, he began to discuss his own experiences more freely, too.

My parents held me up when I could no longer walk; when, night after night, I would sob that I couldn't face another day, they would listen and comfort me, not allowing their own fears for my sanity to surface.

I have three extraordinary girlfriends, all of whom, in their very different ways, helped me to limp from day to day. They all knew that I didn't want to talk to anyone, apart from Mum and Dad, but nevertheless they phoned every day with the same message: 'I love you and I'm with you.' Each message relayed by Mum made me cry. The father of one of my friends was terribly ill with cancer and I had to tell her that I couldn't be there for her, I could offer no support or love or practical help as I had none left to give. She was utterly understanding and, despite her own personal anguish, still managed to comfort me with affection and support. Another one of my three angels spends her life travelling the world and each day I would have a call from the furthest ends of the earth just to say 'hello'; and my last, faithful girl would drive a hundred miles to come with me for a dog walk, just to hold my hand and hug me tightly.

My cousin had suffered with clinical depression for many years and when she heard that I was ill she came to visit. Talking to her that day was a huge breakthrough for me. She understood exactly what I was going through; she could empathize with my errant mind as she had gone through a similar experience when she wanted to scream hysterically for the noise in her head to stop. She encouraged me to look at my photographs of happier times, birthdays and holidays, days when I was carefree and laughing, a reminder that there was a time when I had been happy and not submerged in my warmth-less world. Most importantly, she promised me that one day the sun would glimmer from behind the dark clouds and, slowly, I would emerge from the gloom.

Back in my own tumultuous world, I was amazed, staggered, angered and upset by the reactions that I received from some friends and work colleagues who knew about my illness. One particular friend's reaction I will never forget. A week after Christmas I phoned her and said that I wasn't very well. Always dramatic, she said, 'Oh my God, what's wrong?' When I told her that I had clinical depression she replied with, 'Oh, I thought it was something serious.' I felt as if I'd been slapped in the face. Then there was a friend of my Mum who suggested that I should 'eat more bananas', apparently a wonderful cure for depression. Someone else said, 'I think I was depressed once.' Several people said, almost accusingly, 'Well you look OK.' How was I supposed to look? How should anyone with a mental health problem look? I soon came up with an answer: 'I haven't lost a limb; I've just lost my way.'

The previous year I had a malignant melanoma removed from my left thigh. The procedure of diagnosis, removal and biopsy was very straightforward and explained in great detail by a consultant. When I was diagnosed with clinical depression, there was no such explanation. There was no quick fix, no wonder drug, no timescale as to how long the illness would last. I couldn't have the malignant part of my brain, which was causing me so much anguish, cut out – unlike the poisonous mole. The canker in my head was unseen, ominous and threatening. Whilst recovering from the six-inch hole in my leg, I was inundated with cards and phone calls, flowers, visits from friends and the support and encouragement from dozens of people.

Whilst battling my depression in those tortuous early days, there was nothing but silence. People left me alone, not knowing how to react to the news of my illness. My three closest friends, and my parents, were the only ones who seemed to care. I felt even more alone and isolated.

I wanted to scream that my illness wasn't contagious or terminal or something to be ashamed of. All I longed for was understanding and not the strange looks that people, who I thought I knew so well, cast upon my wan, unsmiling face. Depression is a silent illness, not a physical illness: it is like an unseen broken neck and just because it can't be seen doesn't mean that it is not as insufferable as physical pain.

But if I was finding the illness difficult to fathom myself, how could I possibly expect others to understand? When Dad had been ill, for the second time, I remember being frustrated with him and not being able to comprehend what he was going through. I was working full-time and, due to the nature of his depression and acute anxiety, I was often tied to the house to look after him which in turn impacted on my own life. Selfishly, I didn't give him the patience and understanding that I now so desperately craved myself. I now know what he went through; I can understand the severity of his illness, and also the inability of others to be sympathetic and supportive. If it was confusing for those around me, it was a damn sight more confusing for me. One of the worst effects of clinical depression, or perhaps of any mental health illness, is that the sufferer feels that they are not who they once were. I was subdued, lethargic and reclusive, and any form of pleasure, even the ability to smile, had vanished from my shipwrecked mind. I lost me. All that was left was a battered soul and an empty heart. I was rudderless, adrift on an ocean of uncertainty.

Some of my friendships grew stronger; as I have said, my three girlfriends never ceased in their steadfastness and love. Sadly, some friendships fell by the wayside – I didn't have the emotional stamina to sustain relationships which were one-sided and a drain on my fragile feelings. One friend who I had always considered to be rather special disappointed me enormously. She came to visit, and as I sat with her over a cup of tea in the kitchen, sobbing silently, she told me that she couldn't cope with my illness, that she had lost a great friend. That wasn't what I needed to hear – I so desperately needed her understanding and support, I wanted her to hug me and tell me that I would get better, that she would always be by my side. But she could only think of herself and how my illness was affecting her. Over the coming months, I slowly cut the ties of our friendship, a painful process but one which was important for my mental well-being. I had spent so much of my life trying to be a good friend, listening to others and propping them up through divorces, deaths and all of life's obstacles, but now I needed my friends to help me. It was those that I least expected to understand who stood firm and loyal, and the friends who I thought would give me strength were too consumed with their own lives to care. As one friend from America wrote, 'You have been bailing out the boat while other people have been chopping holes in the bottom for so long – and it's staggering how many people you kept afloat.'

A week after seeing my psychiatrist, a cognitive behavioural therapist called me at home. She sounded friendly on the phone – quietly spoken, polite and confident that CBT would be able to help me. We arranged an appointment for the following Friday. It was 8 February 2006, six weeks after my breakdown. CBT challenges the way you think and behave, breaking problems down and focusing on the here and now.

Mum insisted on coming with me for company on the seventy-mile round trip. Rather pent up with nervousness and anxiety, I set off for the coast. We arrived with ample time to spare, and Mum did her best to calm my fractious nerves with a flask of tea and Mars bars. Eventually, I went into the clinic and waited for the therapist. When she walked into the reception room, I was immediately relieved. She had a warm smile and was about my age. She was normal! I don't know quite what I had expected, but

I guess I had a preconceived idea of what a 'therapist' should look like – a misconception brought about by too many episodes of *Frasier* and the general idea that you lie on a couch, pouring out your problems whilst a bored looking therapist with a beard and spectacles nods sagely in the corner.

And so started my CBT – over the next two years I saw my therapist regularly. At first I would see her each week and latterly every two weeks. She managed to unravel the knots in my brain with gentle persuasion, expertise and understanding.

She saw me in my most vulnerable state. There were sessions when I could barely speak – the tears would consume me and I would just listen and nod. Each night I would write how I was feeling in my diary. My journal became an important place where I could be completely honest, noting the most painful experiences of the day, an outpouring of my innermost thoughts. I would read excerpts from the diary to my therapist during our sessions – it was the easiest way to explain how I was feeling. I had never written a journal before but I had a great need to record what I was going through, and it has become an important reminder of the day-to-day struggle with my illness.

The most important advice that my therapist gave me was that depression is a self-limiting illness and, in time, I would find a way through the mental agony. Many, many times I argued with her, disbelieving her conviction, but still she persisted, and she was right. To this day, if my mood plummets, I remember her words.

Even though the sessions were exhausting, I always

came away with an insight into how my muddled brain worked; what my distorted beliefs were and how much damage they had done to my psyche; how I saw myself; how I could change my way of thinking from irrational to rational. My sessions allowed me to empty my brain – rather like emptying a handbag. I could throw all of my thoughts at the therapist and she would disentangle and make sense of them. Apparently, we have an average of 60,000 thoughts a day – well I was probably having 600,000, my brain was so out of control. She unlocked my mind and gently peeled back the layers of my soul. She gave me confidence and self-respect; she challenged my negativity; she taught me how to look after *me*; she helped me to change my way of thinking. After forty years of self-doubt, my therapist opened my eyes and, although it took countless hours of intense therapy, I trusted in her to take a leap of faith and face my future with a new-found confidence.

Looking back, with the help of her experience and wisdom, I can understand why I became smothered in a long depressive illness. When you put yourself under such unendurable pressure, and life is devoid of self-belief, you can only sink ever deeper into a quagmire of confusion, finding yet another hidden depth of angst in which to hide. It was painfully difficult for me to change when I had lived by certain rules for most of my life and to accept that, while those rules did help to protect me from my most negative beliefs, ultimately they were unrealistic and destructive. You are led to believe, by your own way of thinking, that what you perceive is absolutely true and you could not possibly think in any other way. If you have never challenged your beliefs and your way of thinking, how can you possibly expect to change?

And how do you find the courage to make that change?

My limitations remained, however; I couldn't concentrate when watching television; I was apt to put my clothes on inside out; I couldn't understand the simplest of recipes; I forgot birthdays and couldn't remember conversations or telephone numbers; I'd drive to the village and then come home, forgetting the reason for my visit. Once, I drove the seventy miles to see my therapist, only to find that I had the wrong day.

I tried to read every day, but more often than not I had to read chapters twice for the words to register in my brain. To try to focus my brain on my morning walk, instead of shuffling along, walking head down, I took a small notebook with me and would write about my observations. I would note when I saw the first bluebell of spring or the crab apples in autumn; observed the ferns beginning to unfurl or the cones falling from the pine trees; or heard the bellowing of rutting deer. By looking in close detail at what was happening on the outside, I diverted my attention away from what was happening on the inside and the multiplicity of my sorrows.

My therapist asked me to write an activity schedule on a weekly basis. The first week I completed my task, but I felt deeply ashamed. Before my breakdown, every minute of my day had been busy, but now my days were meaningless. The daily routine consisted of my dog walk, a sleep, lunch, another sleep, dinner and then bed. Day after day. I had no energy. I tried to run, but didn't get to the end of the road; I tried to swim but barely got to the far end of the pool; I tried to do yoga but I found the soft music and the chatter unbearable. And then it dawned on me – if my mind cannot function how the hell could I expect my body to work? With a physical illness it's the body that suffers and more often than not the brain is still functioning perfectly normally. But if my brain was in such a dislocated state that I couldn't even put my clothes on the right way round or read a chapter of a book, how could I expect it to send the right signals to my body? With this discovery I dismissed my proverbial hair shirt and accepted the fact that my body and mind needed time to heal.

With knowledge and hindsight, I now know that my mind could no longer function in the normal way because the illness had scrambled my brain's chemical balance and my hundred billion brain cells were in chaotic disarray. The signals in my brain were now defunct. Rather like train tracks leading into a large station, if the points are in the wrong place and the trains are at the wrong platforms, and there are trains waiting to arrive, chaos will erupt. And that's what had happened inside my head.

My psychiatrist patiently told me, repeatedly, that certain chemicals in my brain, noradrenaline and serotonin, were drastically depleted and I needed these chemicals for my brain to function efficiently. Therefore, I needed to take medication that would increase production of these fiendish chemicals to resuscitate the process. There is no quick fix for depression and there is no time limit for the illness. People respond differently to different drugs and, because there is so little known about how the brain actually works, it is impossible for the experts to formulate a drug to suit all. Dad and I have a different cocktail of antidepressants, each prescription tailored to our individual needs.

Unfortunately, there is no medical test for depression. Blood tests, scans or X-rays cannot detect the illness so it all comes down to the medication and time. It is strange that in our rapidly changing world we have conquered outer space but not our inner space.

It would be a tortuously long time before we got the medication right. In fact, it was two years before my depression finally succumbed to lithium, a drug I had so strongly objected to previously. I had thought that lithium was a 'last resort' drug, a pill for manic depressives, a drug that made you into a zombie. After much persuasion over many months, my psychiatrist (who firmly believed that the drug would be beneficial to me) finally convinced me to take it. For me, it really was a last resort: I had reached a plateau and felt stuck; my mood had improved marginally but I clearly needed more medication to enable me to move forward. I would need to have blood tests every three months to monitor my thyroid and kidneys, which could both be damaged by the lithium, so it was a decision that I struggled with for some time. Lithium can also conjure up some rather unpleasant side-effects but, fortunately for me, it was the one drug that didn't affect me physically.

Eventually, I was taking three antidepressants: lithium, an SNRI and mirtazapine.

The SNRI and mirtazapine conjured up some terrible side-effects. As well as the constant constipation, the most unbearable were hallucinogenic dreams, together with a permanently dry mouth, swollen joints and weight gain. I did learn to live with each impediment, convincing myself that anything was better than the days of dark despair.

But I did struggle with the weight gain. My therapist and I were really working hard at trying to improve my body image and the way in which I saw myself, so when I began to pile on the pounds we began fighting a difficult battle. And other people's comments, once again, were like poisoned barbs. On one occasion a particularly unkind neighbour took hold of one of my many stomachs and thrust her whiskery face in mine: 'Put on a bit of weight, have we?' I was mortified. It was, undoubtedly, the most unkind and tactless comment, and one which sent me crashing into self-loathing and excruciating shame.

Eight months after my breakdown, I spent a week in Devon with one of my three girlfriends and her two children. Whilst walking along the beach one day, her ten-year-old son made an extraordinary observation: 'You always used to be three minutes ahead of everyone else, and now you're one minute behind.' He was absolutely right and both my friend and I looked at him in astonishment. I was always running at full pace, miles ahead of anyone, metaphorically running as fast as I could so that no one could catch up with me, or, more importantly, so that I couldn't catch up with myself. Before we went to Devon, I watched the video from the previous year's holiday in Pembrokeshire. I barely recognized the loud, over-exuberant, funny, mad redhead on the screen. Had I always been like that? The answer, according to my friend, who I had known for thirty years, was emphatically yes. I would rev the children up into a frenzy, plan the holiday like a military exercise, never allotting relaxation time or time for sitting still on the beach. I had an abundance of energy which was infectious, but no one could match my pace. I was like a greyhound on speed. And now, I had crashed to a halt. In Devon I had no energy to play tennis or swim or surf or play with the children. I dragged along behind them in a daze. I left all of the decision-making up to my friend and just meekly followed her lead. I had metamorphosed from an express train to a snail.

One of the most interesting aspects of my illness was learning people's perception of me before I was ill. My osteopath told me that he didn't feel that he had ever really known the real me – I was always humorous, albeit dripping with sarcasm, and never spoke about myself, evading any personal questions. When I was ill he remarked on how much calmer and more honest I was, with no barriers or pretences to mask what was going on inside. One of my new-found friends, who didn't know me before I became ill, said that she could see that 'the mist was clearing', that I no longer seemed so troubled behind my eyes.

So, four years later, where am I now? Well, I have good days, bad days and indifferent days just like everyone else. Sometimes the bad days are like vicious bites on the bum – and have a tendency to drag my mind back to those ominous, dark days of despair. And when those days consume me the hours aren't as desolate, desperate and mentally destructive as they once were, and I hold on to my therapist's words, 'It will pass. You've been here before,' or to Winston Churchill's famous maxim, 'We must just KBO [keep buggering on].'

I no longer feel any remnants of shame that I have clinical depression. It is not an illness to be ashamed of – rather one that warrants understanding and empathy.

As time marches on, the bad days become less odious and less frequent. I smile more now and laugh spontaneously, and the smile on my face no longer feels strange. For some unknown reason, I still can't listen to music and have no desire to, and I still have a strong aversion to noise, always jumping out of my skin when I'm startled. Looking back, I think there was so much noise in my head, rather like a radio which isn't tuned in properly, that now I have to have relative quiet and calm in the space between my ears.

Now I'm a gardener which suits my soul perfectly. I'm outside, on my own, in the fresh air and nurturing my clients' gardens throughout the seasons. I've learnt a lot about horticulture and have marvelled at the wonder of nature. I've seen flying hedgehogs and cart-wheeling grannies; been chased by a pregnant cow and a herd of sheep; been stalked by a toad; toppled backwards into a pond; driven a lawnmower over a stone wall; had my lunch stolen by donkeys; fallen headfirst into a compost bin; and encountered snakes and frogs (both reptilian and human). I've had the luxury of time to stand and study the extraordinary lifestyles of swallows, watched owls hunting in the dusk and rescued baby hedgehogs. I've gazed, in awe, at herons and kingfishers, buzzards and sparrow-hawks.

To my absolute delight, I've seen bulbs that I've planted burst into vibrant life at the dawn of spring; tomato plants that I have grown from seed weighed down with burgeoning fruits; sweet pea plants that I have nourished smothered in scented blooms. Plants that have been moved have flourished under my watch and some that have perished have not withered in vain as I have learnt from my mistakes and experiments.

Physically, my gardening has been a great benefit to my health. My bingo arms have vanished through endless hours of sweeping leaves and mowing lawns. My bottom is no longer like a blancmange and my hair is streaked with tints of golden sunshine. The fresh air and the quiet solitude have helped me slowly to piece together the fragments of my life. The earth has grounded me and the quiet sounds around me have nursed my fragile senses. Even the gentle autumn rain and the biting north wind have brought me solace and calm.

The chaos has vanished from my life for the first time in forty years. I work for some delightful people who have no hidden agendas. They don't put me under pressure or make demands; they simply want to enjoy their gardens and are happy for me to do the hard work!

Life is much more manageable and simpler now. Some friends have fallen by the wayside, but others have popped up like the first primroses of spring and they bring simplicity and honesty, laughter and balance to my days.

I no longer feel the necessity to please those who can never be pleased, only those who it is a pleasure to gladden. I am equipped with my artillery of CBT techniques which prop me up when I feel vulnerable and, together with my new self-confidence, I am stronger and more at peace within myself than I have ever been. I am no longer afraid of life and now have the courage to really *live* life. I am older, wiser and calmer.

After one of my sessions with my therapist I wrote on a piece of card: 'Every waking moment and every breath I take belongs to me.' It is my personal mantra, which I live by every day.

Once again, my morning walks are a delight and the most important part of my day. Bella died at the age of twelve and left rather large paw prints behind, which my new dogs are trying to fill. We wander and ponder through the woodland and heathland, watching deer and noting nature's daily surprises. I earn little money, but I no longer yearn for designer handbags and fancy shoes, mostly because I spend my time in wellies. I no longer hide behind a mask of heavy makeup or am bedecked in jewellery; I don't even wear a watch as I have no timetable to live by. I may not be my ideal weight but I am on medication which causes weight gain and slows down my metabolism, a condition that I have to live with.

I've picked up my camera again and continue to take endless photographs of dogs, flowers, wildlife and my woods, which are a constant source of pleasure to me.

In the last four years I have learnt more about myself and human nature than I could ever have hoped for.

I am forty-three years of age and my future belongs to me – I am in control of it. *I own me*. I can never go back to life before depression – it was too chaotic and now I don't feel the need to run away from myself. Rather like the Wizard of Oz, I was hiding behind a fake persona,

a larger-than-life figure who pretended to be indestruct-
ible.

Now is the time to step forward, to be brave, to slay my
fears and conquer my anxieties; to set my mind and soul
free, and allow myself to soar to the heights that I deserve
and which no longer petrify me. I need to put my life back
into order and maintain a healthy mind which is no longer
a prisoner of plaguesome demons. I am still on medication
for clinical depression and have accepted the fact that the
longer I continue to take the antidepressants, the less
chance there is of a relapse. The tablets keep the darkness
harnessed and out of sight.

Sir Edward Dyer (1543–1607) wrote an extraordinary
poem called 'My Mind to Me a Kingdom Is'. It has become
a favourite of mine, especially two lines:

> *But all the pleasure that I find,*
> *Is to maintain a quiet mind.*

He could have written that for me.

2

Feeling the feelings

I was generally quite a happy child and I grew up in quite pleasant surroundings; my dad was a lawyer, I went to a private school and we lived in a nice house in a good area. Like any other kid, I greatly enjoyed playing with my friends. I always had quite a vivid imagination and really liked playing different characters in games. I would dream of being a performer on stage as an adult. Every schoolteacher would say in my report that I was a bit of a daydreamer as my attention would often wander away from what was going on in class, preferring to look at the trees out the window. However, in general, I was always very well behaved, did all my homework and rarely got into trouble either at home or at school. I was a perfectionist and would have top marks for my schoolwork, a tidy room and hair perfectly groomed into a side-parting, loaded with my mum's hair mousse! I think some of these characteristics did not make life easy when adjusting to the reality of becoming an adult.

I think I started to have feelings of low mood and depression when I was in my teens. Perhaps this was because I found the transition into becoming an adult quite difficult. Being a teenager isn't easy for anyone, but any added problems during this time can make it all the more difficult. I think I got a hard hit of reality that made me realize how much of an imperfect world we live in. The experiences at this time shattered the idyllic picture of the life I had dreamed I would lead as an adult.

Around this time I had begun to discover my sexuality. From a very young age I always knew I felt differently towards boys. I even remember playing 'tig' at kindergarten and rather enjoying chasing the Primary 7 class monitor around the playground. I was always determined to be the first to catch him! However, whilst I always had these feelings I knew instinctively that I should never tell anyone. As a teenager, I remember being horrified coming to the realization one night that my thoughts about boys in fact meant I was 'gay'. The only people I could think of who were gay were flamboyant celebrities like Boy George and Jimmy Somerville. I couldn't see how I related to them. I think having these feelings gradually made me feel very alone and different from my peers. They were becoming increasingly more interested in girls and would go out on the pull to the under-eighteens' nights in town. I once joined them and was thankful that none of the girls were interested in me. They clearly didn't find my Disney sweatshirt and side-parted hair too sexy!

At the same time I was being bullied at school. In science class the group of boys who sat behind me would throw staples into my hair, much to the entertainment of the rest of the class. I could never figure out what it was about me that made me such an easy target. I was really quiet and kept myself to myself, trying my best to remain invisible. I don't think the geeky hair helped though! What was worse was being bullied by the other kids who got bullied themselves. This made me feel as though I was right at the bottom of the pecking order! Every time someone called me a poof I would go home feeling really low and eat excessively to calm the feelings. I was no good at sticking up for myself and assumed it would only make it worse. I didn't see the point in going to teachers about it because I thought that would make me seem weaker. Gradually I really withdrew into myself and became a bit of a loner as a teenager.

I thought there must be something fundamentally wrong with me for people to think they could treat me that way. At the time I wasn't sure why but, looking back, I think it was clear that I was different from the other boys. I also had different interests and felt pressure to conform. I was forced to play rugby at school because I was quite tall and broad. I began to dread weekly rugby practice and would spend entire games trying to keep as far away from the ball as possible. I think that most of all I feared messing up my hair! I also felt I could never tell my dad that I hated going along to watch football matches. I would fall asleep in a throng of chanting supporters. Joking aside, I was always aware that who I really was had to be kept a secret. I think this fear of rejection and efforts to please people became an ongoing pattern that would cause bigger problems in the long term.

My father was also having problems at work and developed an alcohol problem. He would disappear on binges and then come home and collapse on the living room floor in a drunken stupor. A couple of times we had to call an ambulance because he seemed unconscious. He lost his job and we had to move to a much smaller house. My dad had always been a very kind, gentle man and it really upset me to see him in such despair. It seemed like he had a breakdown almost overnight and I think this really threatened my sense of security. However, it sounds strange but at the time I was feeling quite low and I remember thinking this now gave me a reason for feeling the way I did. It all really took a toll on my mum and the house no longer seemed a warm, loving environment like it had before.

When it came to leaving school and deciding what to do with my life I felt as though I wasn't allowed to make my own decisions. My parents had invested thousands in my private education and wanted me to pick a career that provided a good steady income. It seemed as though I was presented with limited options: law, medicine or accountancy. Everyone else at school seemed to be in the same position, with their parents hoping that they would follow a similar professional career path to themselves. I think this made the expectations put upon me seem normal, making it harder to question whether I had any choice.

From a young age I knew that I wanted to be on stage. I dreamed of it day in and day out. When I presented this to my parents it was met by laughter. They told me that I had to be realistic about my options. I thought they didn't care whether a job made me happy or not. I hadn't really had much experience of performing because it was always perceived as something girls did – boys played football. Besides, I didn't have the confidence and the thought of getting up on stage was something that filled me with dread. I joined a drama group and was told that I played the part I was given in quite a camp way. This confirmed my worst fears and I decided that the reality of getting up and performing was much less enjoyable than the dream that was in my head. For these reasons, my performing dreams started to fall by the wayside.

In a desperate attempt to get my parents to support my career choice I decided use some emotional bribery and come out to them as gay. I figured that they might feel sorry for me and support me in what I wanted to do. I couldn't have got a worse reaction. They were having a lot of their own problems at the time and I was met with 'How could you do this to us?' They thought that I had perhaps been influenced by CDs I was listening to or magazines I was reading. They thought that if anything a career in the performing arts would only make me 'more gay'. I felt extremely alone and angry.

I remember that at this time I began to get tension headaches and started to experience feelings of depression that wouldn't go away. I felt trapped and couldn't find a way out. I was so tired of fighting and thought it was easier to just do what my parents wanted me to do. So I studied law to please my parents. It was the shortest of the professional courses and apparently offered a broad range of skills. However, at the same time, I was all too aware that it wasn't going to land me a glamorous role in a hit American court drama! I figured I would run away at the end and do what I wanted to do. I just bottled up my feelings and got on with it. I didn't realize, though, how much an effect this would have on me in the longer term.

University became a fog that I felt trapped in. I remember thinking that going to university should be exciting – a time of freedom and fun. Instead I felt like I was being dragged through life by other people's expectations. I recall sitting in my first law lecture and thinking I had absolutely no interest in what was being talked about. I still stayed in the closet and began to date girls. It sounds strange, but I think girls finding me attractive gave a boost to my self-esteem that I needed at the time. I had been taking medication that really helped me with my acne and I thought it was amazing that girls found me attractive. Also, pulling girls proved to all the people who had bullied me at school that I wasn't the poof they thought I was. Despite this, I couldn't help but feel I was living a life that was one big lie.

So I decided one night to go to a gay club in a different city, completely alone. I met a guy and ended up seeing him for a bit. He dumped me when he realized I was nineteen and closeted. I had never felt more alone. However, I gradually made some friends on the gay scene and started going out. I hoped at the time that doing this would perhaps make me happy but I found it all really seedy and I just got even more depressed. Despite this, I continued to go out on the gay scene a lot and drinking would give me three- to four-day hangovers, which only made me feel a lot worse. I began to tell friends I was gay and found some things really difficult. I thought everybody was gossiping about me.

I felt as though I had no control over my destiny and nobody to turn to. I detached from everything and reached an all-time low. I had gone from being an organized and motivated student at school to not turning up for lectures and handing essays in late at university. I just felt numb. I think my parents thought that I was just a typical lethargic student. A lot of my friends had similarly erratic behaviour. I didn't think I was suffering from depression at the time. However, I didn't realize was that what I was going through wasn't typical.

I had a friend at the time who had been open with me about her depression. She too was gay and was going through a period of similarly feeling disillusioned with her sexuality. She described to me how she was unable to concentrate long enough to watch a whole film. I felt as though I understood what she was saying as my concentration levels were really poor and I was becoming quite forgetful. She mentioned that she had been on medication and how it had helped her. I expressed my own worry about how I was feeling and she encouraged me to do something about it.

I decided to go to my doctor. I explained what was happening at the time and he prescribed an antidepressant to help me through this difficult period, but he didn't mention any other therapies like counselling. I remember feeling a sense of relief that the way I was feeling wasn't normal. Being diagnosed with depression gave me hope that life wasn't supposed to be this way. I thought that the medication would be the solution to all my problems. However, with time I found that I wasn't really feeling that much better.

I decided to try to get help through my university. I went to the university doctor in the hope that I could perhaps access some extra support services. The doctor I spoke to was really quite patronizing. When I mentioned that I was gay, he seemed keen for me to have a course of hepatitis B injections. I thought that this was irrelevant to me asking for help with my depression – a straight person wouldn't have had this forced upon them and I felt slightly stigmatized. However, despite his attitude, the doctor referred me to the university psychologist. When I had my appointment the psychologist pretty much told me after a ten-minute consultation that I looked fine and didn't really need treatment. I couldn't see how he could tell how I felt on the inside just from looking at me.

This made me feel even worse. I began to doubt my feelings and thought that I was a self-indulgent little brat. I even started to think that the entire situation had been inflicted by my own stupidity. To me, someone who was depressed was unable to get out of bed, very ill and perhaps suicidal. I began to doubt if I was depressed at all. I was managing to scrape by with my university work and none of my friends ever seemed to suspect anything was up. I wondered if maybe life was just hard and this was the way things were supposed to be.

My mum found the antidepressants and sat down to have a chat with me about things. I told her the reason I was taking them was because I didn't know what to do with my life. My dad never spoke to me once about it. I think they just thought it was a phase I was going through. I had opened up to a few friends about how I was feeling and I found that what I told them scared them a bit. One of my friends told me, 'I think you just make life difficult for yourself.' That's the thing with depression: unless you've been through it yourself you find it hard to relate to what someone else is going through. However, I think these reactions just confirmed to me that I just needed to pull my socks up and 'get on with it'.

I continued to take the antidepressants for a full six months despite the fact that they weren't helping in any way, or at least it didn't feel like they were. I continued to see my GP who wasn't particularly helpful and didn't encourage me to try and access any counselling or talking therapy. After the one appointment with the university psychologist where I was told there was nothing wrong with me I went into denial about my problem.

I managed to get through university but found it diffi-cult to cope with my workload. Whenever there came a period where I was under pressure I would be weighed down with negative thoughts. There were real ups and downs. When I finished university I went travelling and had some fantastic experiences. During these times I was relatively happy and the depression would subside a little. However, throughout it all there were still issues that remained bottled up and unresolved.

It wasn't until six years later that I took action to resolve these issues. I was experiencing my worst period of depression. I was working in a job that I didn't enjoy and was staying with my parents after coming back from travelling. I began to suffer from insomnia and would have to drag myself out of bed to go to work after only three or fewer hours of sleep. I would spend hours checking that the windows were closed and the taps were off before going to bed at night. I was very confused and couldn't pinpoint what was causing me to feel so bad. I would lie in bed trying to think of changes that I could make so that I would feel better. However, I felt so low I couldn't think of anything. I had thoughts of suicide and saw it as a possible way out. The idea that it was always an option gave me a sense of relief. I never considered actually acting upon these thoughts but they were definitely there. Over the years what had been a case of mild depression had developed into something a bit more serious. I knew I couldn't continue like this any longer and now there was something fundamentally wrong.

I was reluctant to go back to my doctor as I felt the medication he had prescribed didn't really help. I decided to try out some counselling. I was aware of the waiting lists on the NHS and wanted to take action as soon as possible. I managed to find a local counselling centre that charged a fee based upon what you could afford. Fortunately I was still staying with my parents at the time and could afford a weekly appointment costing £30 a session. At first I found that the counselling really started to open up a lot of feelings I had experienced years ago. I felt as though it stirred up a lot of difficult emotions and made me worse at some points. In particular, it brought out a lot of the anger towards my parents that I had bottled up over the years. This made my relationship with my parents quite difficult for a while. However, talking about these things was a release and I cried for the first time in about ten years. I felt that I was grieving for all that I had been through.

After a few sessions I began to feel very excited about the differences counselling was beginning to make. I knew

I was sorting out stuff that I had been in denial of and had been holding me back for years. Overall, counselling really helped me identify why I was the way I was and what had led me to this point. It also helped me identify the changes I needed to make in my life and in myself. I learnt that I needed to stop trying to please others and learn to please myself. I realized that I had to acknowledge my needs and follow my performing dreams, despite the fact that I was feeling so awful.

I think with depression you just get used to going through life with the blinkers on. The counselling made me realize how strong I had been at just getting on with things and how unhealthy this had really been. I learnt that happiness and sadness go hand in hand. You can't experience one emotion without the other. Bottling things up and not dealing with them just hardens you and stops you from living your life to the full. After every session I felt a real sense of release as though I had really lightened my load. I really felt as though I was starting to feel things again and was ready to move on.

I also had four sessions with a private psychologist. Although the counselling had helped I found it had made me start to ruminate a little too much on things that had happened in the past. My sessions with the psychologist helped me to vent some of my anger towards my parents with letter-writing exercises. She helped me find explanations to resolve how I felt my parents had treated me. She also taught me how to be more assertive with people in order to protect my own self-esteem. Although this was costly I felt that it was worth it. I think I had a lot of regret about not accessing talking therapy earlier and was not prepared to wait much longer. I felt that a short-term investment would possibly reap dividends in the long term. Talking about my feelings and dealing with things I had bottled up gave me a sense of relief. It really made me feel liberated and the more I talked the less numb I felt.

I was still finding my sleep wasn't great at all and I found negative thoughts overwhelmed me at times. Whilst I was starting to have more good days, there were still a lot of bad ones. I then started to receive cognitive behavioural therapy (CBT) on the NHS from a community psychiatric nurse (CPN). I could see from the start that I would probably benefit from CBT. The principles behind CBT – looking at things from an evidence base – made a lot of sense to me. Perhaps my law degree helped me in this respect! I think this positive attitude from the outset allowed me to more fully embrace this form of therapy! Of all the therapists I had seen, I found I had the best relationship with the CPN who took me for these sessions. I think the fact that I liked her as a person made it easier to open up to her. She really encouraged me and made me feel a sense of achievement. That this therapy, unlike some of my previous treatments, was obtained through the NHS shows that you don't necessarily have to pay for the best care.

I began to feel some of the benefits within my first few sessions. I found it helped to curb a lot of the negative thoughts and to see things from a more helpful perspective. It made me realize how I was over-reacting to a lot of things and not seeing things from a realistic point of view. CBT also helped me with my obsession with repeatedly checking things. As I mentioned before I was kept up at night by the need to check things. I was worried that something would go wrong like the house being robbed because a door was left open. This was diagnosed as obsessive compulsive disorder by the CPN and I received treatment that helped me, step by step, to stop checking things. This in turn lowered my adrenalin levels and overall anxiety. Gradually I saw that my general sleep pattern began to improve. This was a big relief because feeling tired all the time is depressing enough in itself.

I also started reading some self-help books. I found that reading them in my spare time not only distracted me from my own thoughts but also made me feel more positive because I was able to do something constructive in my own time. They gave me a relatively cheap way of accessing quality therapy material written by experts in the relevant fields. I was able to obtain some titles through my local library completely for free.

In the course of the different therapies I received I was able to recognize the changes that I needed to make. One thing that emerged was that I needed to move out of my parents' house. Although my parents cared for me they had real difficulty understanding me. As long as I continued to live with them I felt I wouldn't have the space I needed to become my own person. I now visit my parents regularly and have a relationship with them that is based on mutual understanding as respective adults. I now realize that a lot of the problems I had with them was down to generational differences. Their generation believe in the ideal of a good steady job for life and were not exposed to gay people so much because things were not so open. They now accept me more for who I am, albeit they find it hard to understand me. That's OK, as neither do most of my friends after I've had a few beers!

I also started to get back into doing drama and performance. I started singing lessons and joined a local drama group. I really discovered my confidence on stage and was thrilled when the class tutor told me I had a flair for theatre. I felt the magic that sparked inside me whenever I performed. I felt like I had rediscovered something that was so special to me. At this point I acknowledged that this was a part of me that I would be exploring for the rest of my life. Although I had missed out on going to drama school, I felt excited at the prospect of now having the confidence to just get up there and do it. I realized that I could still make it an enjoyable part of my life, even if it isn't necessarily the career path that I end up following. Also, crucially, I felt comfortable enough with my own sexuality and who I was that I didn't care if I came across as camp onstage.

I started to enjoy my independence and found I enjoyed going out with my friends again. I began to love listening to music once more. When I hear the songs I listened to during this period I notice messages in the lyrics that reflected how I felt at the time. I must have subconsciously chosen to listen to those songs because they resonated with how I felt. In particular, the song 'Broken Strings' by James Morrison has a line that goes 'You can play on broken strings, you can feel anything that your heart don't want to feel'. I think this line summed up how I felt at the time I was in therapy. I was feeling feelings that I had bottled up for years and felt broken; despite this I had a sense of hope that I could feel better again. In a sense I hoped that, like the lyrics in this song suggest, my heart could sing again.

After having gone through therapy I felt like I had more of a sense of my true self. I became more aware of who I was and the values I held in life. I became less self critical, cared less about what other people thought and automatically started to stick up for myself a bit more. I noticed a major turning point in myself on one occasion when my aunt, who is known for making quite scathing comments, made some remarks about my weight. I told her that her comments were inappropriate and that she was in no position to criticize. Whilst I am not proud of the fact that I was insulting to her, at the same time I found it remarkable that I was able to do this. Throughout my whole life I have barely said boo to a goose. It showed me that I had a new-found self-respect and expected others to treat me fairly. I still hope to develop my assertiveness further as it is something that does not come naturally to me. I plan to take some assertiveness training in the future that will help me to cement these skills.

I think that depression is something to which I am going to be susceptible. Although I feel much more in control I am all too aware that it could come back. I still do find things tough at times, and when I am feeling stressed my sleep is affected, but I feel much better equipped to deal with my problems. The first thing I do when I start to feel down is take action. This could be by talking to someone, spending more time with friends, reading self-help material or taking more time out to do things I enjoy. I find exercise really helps me. Even when I was feeling really down I found exercise would give me a bit of a boost. The endorphins it produces really help me to get some perspective when things begin to get too much. Through doing these things I am better able to manage my mood and keep myself on track.

My advice to anybody going through a similar experience would be to seek help as early as possible. We live in a culture that still has a 'pull yourself together' attitude when it comes to emotional health. I think other people's reactions, including those of clinical staff, when I first became ill made me think there was nothing wrong with me. I think if you feel there is something not right, it is important to listen to yourself. You may not be depressed, but seeking help early could help prevent you from perhaps becoming ill later.

The most important thing is to get talking. This can be to anyone you trust like a friend or family member, but sometimes it is much easier to say things to someone you don't know and who won't give you their opinion on things. Talking to a counsellor or even someone on a helpline can give you the space you need to think for yourself and find a way forward. When you are depressed it can be really hard to understand your feelings because you feel so numb. I think that when you start talking it becomes easier to identify with your feelings.

I would also encourage someone with depression to not be discouraged by the difficulty in accessing services and the long waiting lists on the NHS. I would advise them to get on the waiting lists and try to access other forms of help in the meantime. There are other things you can do like attend support groups, do free online CBT courses and go to self-help group meetings. If you can afford private treatment then this is also worth considering. There is other help out there through charities and some counselling centres offer sessions for free or based on what you can afford. It can take some time to investigate, but persevere and hopefully you will be able to find things that you can access. Above all, I think it is important to try out a variety of things to find out what works for you as an individual.

My advice for people living with someone who has depression would be to try and be patient, and understand that it is an illness. I would also tell carers for someone with depression to encourage the person to talk about how they feel, and not to judge them or tell them what to do. Sometimes people with depression can push away those close to them. It is important to remember that this is a symptom of the illness and does not necessarily reflect upon the nature of the relationship you have with them.

I now feel much more able to understand my feelings. I try to accept my feelings for what they are and find the best way to cope. I definitely feel stronger for what I have been through. I think I have learnt a lot about myself, life in general and what is important. Despite this I would never wish depression upon anyone. It is really scary and really affects the quality of your life. Unlike some other illnesses there is not one treatment that will work for everyone. It is so complex and individual to the person who has it. I hope that my story encourages anyone who feels that something isn't right to take action. You owe it to yourself to enjoy life as much as you can. I hope my story gives people who are depressed hope that they won't feel the way they do forever. With the right help, it is possible to start to feel again and experience the magic that life can bring.

3

Head against the wall

Discovering I was pregnant came as a bit of a surprise. We had been trying for a baby for quite a few years and had just been referred to a fertility clinic at the local hospital. In fact, I even initially worried that my early pregnancy symptoms were due to a brain tumour, having read somewhere that tumour symptoms occurred in the morning after waking up and gradually got better through the day, and for a while I hadn't even considered the possibility that I was pregnant. I'd recently decided to go freelance from my job as a CD Rom designer/programmer so there would be no maternity pay. When the blue line appeared on the pregnancy detector I was both scared and elated at the same time. When I told him the news over the phone, my husband was delighted and came home from work with a large bunch of flowers for me.

The pregnancy passed in a completely normal way. I went through the same period of worries that most women who are pregnant for the first time go through. I was excited and couldn't wait to meet this little person growing inside me. I was also worried about how I would cope with being a mother. I was, by then, in my thirties and had spent my twenties vehemently insisting that I didn't want children, preferring instead to engage in a boisterous social life of pubs, music gigs, restaurants and parties. I got married when I was in my late twenties but it was a few years before I began to wonder about becoming a mother. The relationship with my husband was the first one in which I could believe that we had a future together and having children seemed naturally to be the next step. The only problem that developed during the pregnancy was that I have a backwards tilting uterus and was carrying the baby in the breech position, up-side down and feet first. The baby was also facing my spine rather than facing outwards as in a normal pregnancy. I was told that I would have to have a caesarean. I wasn't actually bothered about this; in fact, I thought that having the baby surgically removed sounded better than giving birth naturally. I wouldn't have to do all the work.

The caesarean was booked for when I was thirty-eight weeks pregnant but I went into labour a week earlier and had to have an emergency caesarean instead. I had woken up that morning with bad stomach cramps and knew that I was in labour. The cramps continued regularly all day as I determinedly ignored them; being someone who hates hospitals, I waited until the last possible moment to telephone them and get myself there. I could have gone to the hospital any time during the day because I had to have the caesarean; I didn't really need to wait until I was fully ready to give birth as a woman having a normal delivery would. It was a Friday and I had organized a 'Last View of the Bump' party for Saturday night. Even whilst know-ing that the party almost certainly wouldn't now happen

– I was having fairly regular contractions all day – I went on shopping as if it would. It was after midnight when I finally telephoned the hospital. Perhaps, looking back, this shows that I still hadn't come to terms with the massive change in my life that was about to happen.

Due to my reticence, the anaesthetist had to be paged out of bed at 2 a.m. and only a small group of night staff were available on the wards. I walked into the operating theatre where I was given a spinal anaesthetic to numb me from the chest down and the process of my becoming a mother began. My daughter was born at 4.27 a.m. and I was overjoyed to meet her. After I gave her a kiss, the theatre nurses took her to be checked and weighed. She was tiny and weighed just 5 lb but she was the most perfect baby I had ever seen. I was officially in love.

Things began to go wrong when I was wheeled into the recovery room. After a caesarean operation, women are given an epidural to keep them pain free for the first twenty-four hours after surgery. In my case it didn't work and sensations of pain began to prickle around my abdomen immediately after the anaesthetic had worn off. By the time I was taken to the ward, I was in agony and had to be given regular injections of morphine to stop the pain. My husband stayed with me and we spent most of the morning talking about and cuddling our new daughter. Although I hadn't slept all night and was in considerable pain, I was feeling ecstatic about my little baby and even had her tucked up in bed with me for a while. Eventually, around lunchtime, my husband left so that I could get some sleep. From that point onwards, things went rapidly downhill.

I later learned that the fact that the twenty-four hour anaesthetic hadn't worked was not written on my medical notes. When the nurses changed shifts at lunchtime the new staff had no idea why I was in so much pain because no one had told them – they treated me as a nuisance. I was only allowed to sleep for an hour and then was forcibly woken up and pulled into a sitting position. The pain was so bad after being manhandled in that way that I was in tears and the nurses were rude and uncaring; in their ignorance they couldn't believe that I was in so much pain. I was exhausted, having only slept for one hour in forty-eight hours. There was no explanation given as to why I was woken up so roughly. The injections of morphine continued along with a dose of antiemetic each time because morphine causes nausea and vomiting. However, you can have more morphine than the antiemetic and eventually the morphine injections were making me vomit. When I started to feel sick, I rang the bell for the nurse who didn't turn up for about five minutes. She arrived impatiently as if reluctant to be at work and when I told her that I was about to be sick, she handed me my water jug and said, 'Use that,' before walking away. By the time my husband returned to visit me he was shocked at the state he found me in after leaving me in such an elated mood earlier in the day. I still don't know if my treatment in hospital contributed to the way I eventually began to feel. Throughout all this, however, I loved my daughter deeply and holding her in hospital always improved my spirits despite the overworked and testy nurses. When I was allowed to go home three days later I felt happy and excited about taking my baby home.

On the way home we sat in the back of a taxi as I carefully held our little girl to keep her safe. Once home, we placed her in a Moses basket bought for us by my sister-in-law and watched her sleep. I was so relieved to be away from the hospital and looking forward to getting back to normal. I still hadn't realized that what I called 'normal' wouldn't be a condition I would be returning to any time soon. Perhaps another illustration of what my previous normal life was like came in the form of a large bottle of vodka, bought for me as a present after giving birth, by two close friends (they didn't have children). It would be some time before I drank that vodka.

At the time, we still lived in a one-bedroom flat in London and in order to ensure that we could get at least some sleep each, we bought an inflatable bed to put in the living room. That first night I suggested that I sleep on the mattress and my husband sleep in the bedroom. Because our daughter was so tiny I had been advised not to take her outside during the cold weather (it was November), and we had a very cold bedroom at the back of the flat so I was worried about her getting cold. The living room had a warm fire and I was still in fearsome 'mother lion' mode; I was going to look after my own baby myself and in my own way. Most new mothers are full of such paranoia and worries: all you can think about is looking after your baby, terrified that something bad might happen to them. When we had the idea for the sleeping arrangements, I had never had a caesarean and had no idea how much pain I would be in afterwards. Just the very act of trying to sit down on a mattress on the floor was agonizing. It is in my nature to just carry on regardless, a strength I'd always been proud of, so I just lay down and carried on. I was up almost every twenty minutes that first night and I honestly can't say which was worse, the pain or the sleep deprivation.

The next day my husband went back to work leaving me on my own with the new addition to our household. I have spoken with friends who have since had caesarean births and they've all looked at me open-mouthed when I told them that from the first day out of hospital, I was looking after my baby alone. I had always been someone who strives to be very capable and independent. The thought of asking anyone for help horrifies me; my personal silent mantra, 'I can manage', is only ever a thought away. But almost everyone I've met who has been in that situation has needed someone to help them. For six weeks, you are not allowed to drive, lift anything heavy, walk too far or even clean your home. Telling me that I was, in effect, helpless was one of the worst things that could happen to me; being vulnerable was never a condition in which I'd expected to find myself. In this new life I was told I must be needy – this was not only alien to me, it was also very distressing. From then on, little pockets of darkness began to infiltrate my mind.

During the day I would sit with my daughter in the living room. All my friends were at work and I have no family in London; I was born in Manchester which is where all my family still live. It was the time of year when it goes dark at 3.30 p.m. and back then we didn't have cable or satellite TV. There was nothing for me to do but sit there on my own, exhausted and in pain. I remember panicking because I had no job to go back to, and freelance work was drying up so I had no income either. It felt as if my life had slipped away and there was nothing I could do to get it back. I have never been that close to my mother and so I didn't tell her how I was feeling. In fact, I didn't tell anyone, I couldn't tell my elderly grandmother because I didn't want to upset her, and my sister is much younger than me and it had always been me being supportive of her, never the other way round. For my family, I put on a display of happiness and competence, and they were all suitably impressed, but inside I was becoming increasingly miserable.

I started to have bizarre thoughts about my daughter. There was a strange facial expression she had after being fed and for some reason I began to wonder if she was a demon and causing my unhappiness on purpose. It was only a fleeting thought but it disturbed me because it happened constantly. I did still love her devotedly but was beginning to feel that I really couldn't cope. I resented my husband for having a job and a life outside our tiny flat, people to talk to and the ability to have lunch in a pub or café. My daughter cried constantly day and night. I would make cups of tea and they would be left to go cold because I didn't have time to drink them. In the early weeks after birth, it was just me and my baby in the flat and I began to feel very isolated. My busy life had officially ended and I was alone, housebound.

I stopped tidying the flat and eventually stopped getting dressed and washing my hair. I lost all interest in my appearance. I cried constantly and would start huge rows with my husband. It felt as if my mind was being hijacked by another person. I shouted at my husband, telling him that I hated him when I didn't. I'd shout that I wished that I hadn't had a baby when I actually loved her deeply. I loved both of them but this anger and unhappiness would come over me and I'd start saying things that I didn't mean. I broke most of our crockery one evening in my frustration, most of it thrown at my husband. I was so locked in my misery that I never considered how he must feel about it. I would punch my head or bang it against walls until my face was bruised, punishing myself for being so useless. I had never spent more than two evenings in a row at home and now I was at home twenty-four hours a day. I couldn't go out even at weekends because it hurt to walk and we had no car.

Just before Christmas I received an email from a company that I used to work for inviting me to their annual Christmas party. These were formal affairs involving taxis from the office to a large corporate-style marquee somewhere. I was initially delighted and emailed a former colleague to ask where we would meet. Without me, it was an all-male design team. Instead of replying to my email with a meeting time, his response was, 'What, are you going to bring your baby?' He never did let me know the arrangements so I wasn't able to go. Unsurprisingly, my mood fell even lower after that. We bought a Christmas tree and my daughter loved looking at the lights on it but we didn't go out at all and, for the first time since I was sixteen years old, I spent New Year's Eve at home.

After Christmas, I was finally able to take my daughter outside. We bought one of those little slings and I carried her inside my coat to keep her warm. Being outside really helped me and when I was walking she slept contentedly leaning against my chest so it gave me a little peace too. I decided to join a local baby massage class where there would be other new mothers. However, the whole thing was a nightmare. My daughter hated the massages and screamed blue murder throughout. All the other babies were much larger, even though most were about the same age, and they all gurgled and smiled contentedly – bringing my daughter there disturbed the peace. Another issue was that because of taking medication straight after her birth, I wasn't breastfeeding. To the middle-class women in my neighbourhood this was tantamount to child cruelty and I felt ostracized. Eventually I stopped going to the class. My self-confidence was on the floor by then. Once again my life had been reduced to nothing.

I carried on walking around with my daughter strapped to my body and, although I enjoyed being outside, I still felt very isolated. I remember waking up one day to the sound of loud building work going on. When I looked out of the living-room window I saw that our next-door neighbours were digging a basement beneath their house. We lived in a ground floor flat in a row of tall Victorian terraces and our house had had a problem with subsidence because the whole area is built on clay soil. We had an instrument attached to the wall outside our front door that measured how much the building was moving. I didn't remember any planning permission being asked for. They had just gone ahead with their building plans without telling anyone. That day I found I couldn't open the front door. The doorframe had subsided and the door was stuck. There was no way out of the back garden because we were in a triangle of streets of similar terraces so now I was stuck inside the house for a different reason. These days it's a funny anecdote to laugh about, but at the time I was miserably cursing the neighbours. They had already extended their property so their back door was only four feet from our bedroom wall and the mother would send out her six children into the garden every morning where they made as much noise as possible. We called out a surveyor and the problem was eventually sorted out but at the time, it was just one more thing to drag my spirits down. The lack of consideration by our neighbours increased my feelings of worthlessness. It was as if I wasn't someone whose opinion mattered.

Another issue was the one-bedroom flat that we lived in. It was a housing association flat that I'd got in my twenties but, with three of us living there, the place began to feel very cramped. We contacted the housing association requesting a transfer to somewhere bigger but we were told that a transfer was highly unlikely because they were required by law to give 90 per cent of their available homes to people on the local council's housing waiting list. I felt trapped and once again began crying all the time. At that time we didn't have enough money to buy anything and private rents were so much higher than the flat we had – I couldn't see a way out of the situation. I sunk lower because I didn't have a job and living in a one-bedroom flat with no imminent means of changing the situation made me feel even more helpless. I continued to cry and argue with my husband. One night I threw the remaining crockery at him. My face was again covered in bruises across my forehead from hitting my head against the wall and punching myself. I felt, overwhelmingly, that I couldn't cope any more.

My husband suggested paying someone to help me out for a couple of days a week but I was in such a state by then that I couldn't bear the thought of having anyone around me that I didn't know very well. I felt like I'd stopped being able to communicate with people after spending so many months alone. I also hated the fact that I wasn't dealing with being a mother very well. I was constantly telling myself how useless I was, when I had once been proud of my feisty capability to take on anything. Now I felt as if I couldn't even make a simple meal or manage a conversation.

We had a local wine bar/restaurant that allowed children inside so we began spending our Saturday evenings there. For a while I felt a little better but we soon discovered that the English don't like people with children in their midst when they are out for the evening. If my daughter began to cry we would leave but it wasn't just the tantrums that weren't tolerated – I could understand that – but we were made to feel as if she shouldn't make any noise at all. There was also one particular woman – a regular at the wine bar – who decided to bully me by always rolling her eyes at my clothes as I walked in and talking very loudly about how she worked in a Montessori nursery and I wasn't looking after my baby properly. The old me would have given her a piece of my mind and more besides – I used to be an English and Special Needs teacher and consider myself perfectly educated on how to raise children – but I felt so low that all I could do was feel sad. It started to ruin the one evening of the week when I could have some semblance of my previous life back. I would have stood my ground before my daughter was born but now I retreated into myself. I began drinking at home.

It was around this time that my husband was made redundant. I felt as if I was living in a nightmare with no end to it. It was quite a few months before he got a job in the same industry and, in the meantime, he'd been taking on temping work but the pay was much lower so we had less money to do things at the weekends. It also furthered my feelings of helplessness because I didn't have a job to go back to. I did actually begin applying for jobs but I never got through the interviews. I felt as if I'd lost the ability to communicate and I think the people who interviewed me probably thought I was very odd. I couldn't answer questions properly because my mind wasn't operating rationally: it felt as if I was being interrogated and my response was to close up, so I gave very little of myself to the interviewers. To me it simply felt as if I'd lost everything; no matter how hard I tried I couldn't get the old me back. Now I know that I was depressed but, at the time, I felt that I was officially a waste of space and incapable of taking part in the real world anymore.

My husband began helping by taking over my daughter's care at night. I hoped that getting more sleep might make me feel better but I found that I couldn't sleep anyway. My thoughts and behaviour were so irrational and disordered that I'd get up in the middle of the night and try on my clothes or draw strange things in my sketchbook. There was a white cat that meowed on the bedroom windowsill at about 5 a.m. every morning. I thought that it must have a message for me. I began connecting random events in the belief that I was possessed by something evil that was making me miserable. The rational part of me knew that I wasn't functioning properly. I was still crying every day and punching myself in the head. My forehead was permanently bruised and swollen. I also began drinking heavily. It stopped my mind going over everything that was wrong or how pointless I felt. One bottle of wine became two bottles and I punished myself even more about how useless I was. Eventually, I began to recognize that I needed to do something about what was happening to me. If I went over everything it was clear that I was a long way from being myself. I loved my baby and my husband but something was causing me to behave out of character. I made an appointment to see my doctor.

I was prescribed antidepressants; they were an old-fashioned type that I was to take at night to help me to sleep. Finally getting a diagnosis came as something of a relief. The doctor was very reassuring and told me that there were many treatments to try and I would eventually begin to feel better. Nobody has post-natal depression forever. I was quite willing to try the medication in the hope that it would get me back to being my normal self. Initially nothing happened; I still felt very low and was still finding it hard to cope. After a few weeks, however, I slowly began to feel better. My daughter started to go to a child-minder two days a week, finally giving me some time to myself. I also began to enjoy my time with her much more. As summer progressed I would take her to the park. She was too little to sit on the swings or climb the climbing frame but she loved to watch the older children play. We would go to the paddling pool as the weather got warmer and she'd giggle as I dipped her toes into the water.

Eventually, with my mum's help, we finally got together the money to buy a two-bedroom flat with a garden and I really began to feel as if things were getting better as we planned decorating it and fixing it up. We chose to move away from the area where we'd lived for ten years. I wanted a fresh start somewhere completely different and by the time we moved in I was feeling much more myself. My feisty self reasserted itself and I was able to send our neighbours' children out of my garden (it seemed like they had been using it as the local park) without any problem.

A few years later, I encountered a woman on holiday who reminded me of the woman in the bar we used to go to when my daughter was a baby. My daughter had made some young friends on the aeroplane and was delighted to discover that they were staying in the same apartments as us. On the afternoon of the day that we arrived, I sat reading my book by the pool as she and her little friends played with some kittens. At that point I was the only parent sitting outside watching them. This particular woman seemed to have an issue with me from the outset and began talking loudly about parents allowing their children to mistreat kittens so that they (the parents) could have some peace. We have two cats at home that my daughter has played with since they were kittens and as cat lovers we had taught her to be gentle with them; I couldn't believe what I was hearing and looked up at her.

She gave me a nasty little smirk as if the comments were actually meant just for me. This time I did give her a piece of my mind. I felt that this was a turning point – it really highlighted in my mind how far I had come and that I really was back to my old self.

Looking back I should have asked for help sooner and would urge anyone feeling like I did to see their doctor and admit to at least some family and friends how they feel. It is OK to admit to people close to you that you don't feel all right. Most women do need some sort of help after having a baby. Recognizing this will help you to feel better and will also be better for your baby and those close to you.

4

If at first you don't succeed . . .

Only a few years ago I would never have thought it possible for me to say the following words: 'I find it difficult, now, looking back, to remember in any detail just how terrible I felt at times,' yet this is how I must begin my story. If you are reading this whilst feeling very depressed, please forgive me if I seem to make light of some things – it is not my intention to be shallow or unfeeling, it is simply that I have moved on, my life is full and I am largely happy and content now. My brain seems to have removed the memory of the pain of the years of severe depression much as it has the pain of childbirth; also, as the worst phase of my depression ended around 2001, it is now some distance in the past but, even so, I would like to share my story with you.

In the late 1980s I decided that I ought to find a more lucrative type of work than cleaning and I therefore got a job at the local secondary school as an administrative assistant in the English department. As my first love had always been books and the job was quite varied, I was very happy for a while. Unfortunately this state of affairs did not last. A new Head of Department was appointed who wasn't really up to the job: he wasn't very efficient and was relying on me to help him with many things that were not only outside my remit, but also beyond my understanding and competence. This put great pressure on me, something I have never coped with well, and the resultant stress caused many rather unusual symptoms although, at the time, I just thought that I had a weird virus. I have always put pressure on myself, such as by making up fictitious deadlines to finish something even when it didn't matter at all and trying to be better than everybody else at everything I undertook. This external pressure was new, though – I did not know how to cope with it and, I believe, it stirred up thoughts that I had buried for many years.

I visited my GP who listened to me talk about my mixture of symptoms which included feeling very tired. I didn't want to do anything and didn't really enjoy anything that I did do. I was crying a lot, although as I have always been a very emotional person that hadn't bothered me too much. I was also getting angry with my children more than usual and didn't want sex. The doctor listened very carefully and for a great deal longer than my allotted ten-minute slot, and then said, 'I think you are depressed.' On hearing my doctor's diagnosis you could definitely have knocked me down with a feather. I didn't know that this was only the beginning of many years of illness and horror.

My odd and rather random symptoms were certainly very worrying to me. I had always suffered from a lot of the usual viral illnesses, coughs, colds and suchlike, but I had never lacked motivation or happiness. I was always a very busy person, dressmaking, gardening, doing all sorts of things that amazed my friends whose cry tended to be 'I don't know how you do all these things'. Looking back, it was the feeling of hopelessness that enveloped me that was by far the worse feeling of all. Everyday tasks that I would normally have finished quickly and easily took me ages to complete; even though I had never particularly liked doing housework I had always tackled it as something that just had to be done but now I didn't want to do it at all. I didn't care if the house, myself or even my family were uncared for – nothing seemed to matter any longer. I did the basics as a matter of necessity but took no pride in cooking a nice meal, had no interest in what my children or husband had done each day and became very inwardly focused.

In my mind I felt I knew what everyone thought about me and they were always negative things, that I was too fat, my hair was a mess, I talked too much, I was uninteresting and so on; eventually this led to an enormous drop in my self-esteem although it was all based on erroneous, internal thinking, and not on what anyone had ever said to me. Of course, one of the problems with this type of thinking is that you constantly ruminate, virtually chewing over every thought like a cow chews the cud, and allowing it to reach mammoth proportions. Yet these thoughts were based on absolutely no facts at all. With my mind filled like this there was simply no time or space for anyone or anything else, and I have always felt that my depression was a very selfish illness indeed. In fact, even I found it difficult to describe depression as an 'illness' and I was the sufferer.

I have recently found a very old diary dating from about

1990 – the beginning of my severe depression – that I thought had long since been destroyed along with the many other notes I have written over the years. These short, terse entries give a true idea of the way I was feeling then. I had long since forgotten many of these feelings and I found re-reading some of these entries quite upsetting. They were not written in full sentences – often I was too depressed or anxious to write properly – but this is how they appear in the diary.

So tired, so tense, I withdrew to the bedroom but had to come down to dinner, I could hardly talk.

I feel he [my husband] should hate me, leave me, give up on me.

Feeling weary and worn out. Feeling I want to get away; be by myself.

D [my husband] and the girls have washed, ironed and cooked dinner but it's really taken it out of D and he got upset, this is when I feel that I am not worth his time and trouble and that everyone would be better off without me; he tells me that he must be the judge of that but I cannot accept that.

Didn't sleep too well, was awake from 3 a.m. until 5.30 a.m.

Sent H [my eldest daughter] round to her friend. I've lost most of my friends through this; I can't let her do the same. [This was definitely NOT true, although some of my friends found it difficult to cope not only with the fact that I was ill but also with the type of illness I was suffering from.]

Lost control completely and even thought of suicide

again, D devastated and tried to reason with me but it
didn't work.

Back to this [diary] in the hope of driving devils out
and letting sanity in.

I had a bad attack of feeling useless and that I lacked
self-worth, so bad that I just stood there and cried; I
never used to suffer like this, I accepted what I couldn't
do and always felt I made up for those negatives with
the positives in what I could do well!

This is another diary entry, on a rather more positive note,
to show that even at the worst of times there were
glimmers of light:

I have been able to help D and keep calm which is a real
step forward.

I have sent off my application to Loughborough
University to be a mature student. Decided to have my
hair done, it's been a long time since I felt well enough
to do that.

I hope that this gives you a glimpse of just how I was
feeling at that time. I have to confess that I attempted
suicide shortly after the diary stops. This was the first of
four attempts, each just as horrible in its own way, but the
feelings surrounding each attempt are so difficult to remember. If you have reached those terrible depths of
despair you don't need me to remind you what a nightmare you lived through or are maybe still going through;
obviously if you are reading this you have, like me,
survived, so what you need to know is how to keep going.

But firstly I would like to take you back to the very beginning of my life to understand where my depression originated and to do that I need to go right back to when I was a baby in order to very briefly set the scene. I was born an illegitimate child, in 1951, into a society that had no time nor support for unmarried mothers. My birth mother had what she called a 'wicked' stepmother and was unable to go home so, after my birth in a home for unmarried mothers, she had to leave both her job and her friends and moved in with the parents of a friend in a different part of the country. She managed to keep me in a nursery whilst working full-time, but by the time I was nine months old it had all become too much for her and she put me up for adoption. In her own words 'she wanted a better life for me'; she probably also wanted a better life for herself as she was only twenty-one years old. Some forty years later, when my depression started, I finally felt the first stirrings of abandonment. Why had she kept me and then discarded me? What had I done to make her give me away? I thought that I really must have been a very bad baby.

The adoption went through and I, extrovert that I was, ended up with the most introverted family it was possible to meet. My adoptive father had been a prisoner of war and was quiet and self-contained. My adoptive mother had a very cold nature, possibly due to her own loveless childhood, and I now think that she was also totally repressed; she certainly did her best to repress all my emotions, perhaps because she just didn't understand them – if I laughed I was often told that it would end in tears. My sister, their natural daughter who was six years my senior, resented me dreadfully. I have since learnt from her that she felt that I had been 'chosen', whilst she just 'happened'.

I am now diagnosed as having bipolar disorder (previously known as manic depression). My adoptive mother quoted the following rhyme to me many times: 'There was a little girl who had a little curl, right in the middle of her forehead, and when she was good she was very, very good, and when she was bad she was horrid.' I don't know if I had bipolar symptoms as a child, but I can recall being at both ends of the bipolar spectrum, hence the rhyme; I would spend hours curled up with a book, trying to escape to some magical world that didn't include my adoptive mother, yet did include my birth mother, whilst at other times I would be climbing trees or chasing around on my bike. Perhaps that was simply being normal but I do know that I loved being at school where I could be myself, have lots of friends and learn about all sorts of things – not perhaps the usual attitude to school! You may, of course, think that being 'chosen' would have reassured me, but in fact it was just the opposite. It seemed that every exam I passed, every achievement of mine, somehow became the achievement of my mother because she had chosen me.

So, I began life with two major difficulties, not only being abandoned by my birth mother but also spending my formative years being repressed by my adoptive mother, lacking the cuddles that may have helped me so much. I now recognize I am a tactile, touchy-feely sort of person and probably missed that loving touch more than most. I do remember Mum telling me once that, shortly after going to live with them, I would cry and cry, rocking the cot so violently that it would move across the smooth lino floor. Why I wasn't comforted I have never understood. I have always placed great emphasis on the fact that I was not adopted at six weeks, which was then more usual: at that age a baby would not have made such an attachment to its natural mother. I sometimes think that the comparatively late age of adoption was a major factor in the problems I experienced.

Having said all this, and obviously not knowing anything different, I got on with life and evidently enjoyed everything that I did to the full. Not only did I like school but I found the work fairly easy, but I got little support in my wish to go to university as most of my friends were intending. I left school at sixteen to begin working in a library, the idea being that I would continue studying as well as earning (far more important in my parents' eyes), with a view to going to university later. That just didn't happen and eventually I changed jobs for a better salary. I didn't really like the job at first and almost regretted leaving the library. This was when my first experience of depression was to take place. Although it's so long ago that it's hard to recall my feelings, I know that the company's doctor not only recommended a course of Vitamin B supplements, but also prescribed diazepam, a tranquillizer which was commonly prescribed in the early 1970s but got a very bad press as it was considered to be highly addictive. I cannot have taken it for too long as that did not become a problem. At no time, back in the 1970s, was the term depression mentioned to me.

I had known my husband-to-be on and off since we

were at primary school but when we began to court in the early 1970s I can recall having terrible difficulties with developing a close relationship. At times I used to run away from him whilst out walking: I simply had no experience of being very close to another person and my previously untapped feelings became overpowering. Looking back I now think that I was, in fact, trying to run away from myself, feelings that later found an outlet in my trying the ultimate escape of suicide. I couldn't express the feelings I had for him, but not only did he persevere in those early days, he has stuck by me through some horrendous times since.

We married in 1973 and I found it very difficult to settle into marriage, a new house in a new area with a new job thrown in to boot. I was definitely not mentally well at that time; looking back, the depression was rearing its ugly head again. I couldn't settle into the job and must have had three in the space of that first year of marriage. All I wanted was to start a family, believing that that would help me. My GP at the time, who also never mentioned the word depression, also thought that having a family might mysteriously solve my problems. Of course, there is still stigma attached to depression in the twenty-first century; in the 1970s it must have been far worse so perhaps this is why no one ever used the term with me.

Luckily for me, once we had taken the decision to start a family I became pregnant almost at once and in rapid succession we had three daughters. I really enjoyed being a stay-at-home mum and was in my element making cardboard castles and cooking with the children, but the time came when, as they grew older, we could certainly make use of a bit more money, I'd had some cleaning jobs but now felt that I needed to use my brain a bit more to see if it really still functioned. It was then, in the late 1980s, that I began work at the secondary school and it was while I was working there, and put under so much pressure by the Head of Department, that I was eventually given the diagnosis of depression. This was the first time that the word depression had ever been mentioned to me – luckily I had never suffered from post-natal depression. I did suffer from one or two strange illnesses when the children were young but these turned out to be psychosomatic. It is more than possible that depression was the cause of these but this wasn't mentioned at the time and I usually saw the doctor only for 'normal' illnesses. As had happened before I found that I was trying to escape from my problems by running away, to the extent of hiding in the stockroom or going in a different direction if I knew my new boss was looking for me. I tried to deal with these things and talked to other members of staff who, although sympathetic, were of no practical help. Gradually it got to the stage where I really did not want to go to work. I felt as if I was spiralling out of control; I became less efficient, forgetful and muddled. It appeared that I was taking on the failings of my boss and this was leading to my loss of self-esteem, although this was not a term I had encountered then. When all of this was added to the other symptoms I have already mentioned I decided I had to see my doctor and he gave me the diagnosis of depression. From this time forward I saw my doctor regularly as I began the long road to recovery.

I was not content with a simple diagnosis and I wanted to find out exactly what this thing called depression was. I knew how I felt, of course, but it was very difficult to put into words; Winston Churchill described his depressive times as his 'black dog', but for me it was as if I was at the bottom of a very deep pit, the type that used to be dug by ancient tribes to catch wild animals. Once in I couldn't get out. I could see a glimmer of light at the top of the pit and would shout until I was hoarse but no one ever came to help me. I would try to scramble up the sides of this pit but they were too smooth and I got nowhere. Sometimes a ladder would appear and I might make it up a few rungs but it was always a case of climbing up two rungs and dropping back three, so even when I felt I was getting a bit better, something always happened to drag me back down again.

I had never known of anyone who had suffered from this illness. As I've said it was something not spoken about and was really still considered to be more a case of merely feeling a bit low, having a touch of the blues; in order to get better all you needed to do was to 'pull your socks up'.

I did read some self-help books but they were not terribly helpful, not only because I was still in denial at the diagnosis, but also because most of them were written by American psychiatrists who suggested that you should stick up messages on the mirror, saying things like 'Today you will achieve three things and feel really good about yourself' or 'You are a beautiful person'. This did not go down well with the feelings I was experiencing at the time and also seemed rather alien to the English, somewhat stiff-upper-lip way of approaching things.

Although I obviously did not know it in the early 1990s, depression was to become a feature of my life for many years. Throughout that time, although the basic diagnosis of depression remained the same, sometimes it seemed to become a game of labels and numbers. How many different labels could be attached to one person and their mental condition? In the last twenty years I have had many given to me by different clinicians; they have been no more helpful than the books I initially read. The labels included the obvious 'depression', but also 'anger', 'anxiety', 'SAD' (Seasonal Affective Disorder) and also various personality disorders, the main one being 'Borderline Personality Disorder'. The latter caused me a great deal of distress as it sounded extremely unpleasant. Did I really have such an unpleasant illness? In fact, the labels seemed, at times, to actively worsen my situation as I leapt upon every suggestion, hoping that by having a label I would be able to find at least some answers to my problems. Surely, if someone had created a label, they would understand my problem and therefore be able to help me? However, it didn't seem to work that way: it just seemed to allow the various clinicians I saw to tick the right boxes for their 'in-tray' and then to consign this difficult patient to either the 'dealt with' or 'past hope' tray.

The first difficulty I had was accepting that I was depressed. I had always been a busy, extrovert type of person so I didn't seem to fit the generally accepted pattern of 'the depressed' at all. In fact, once I met an acquaintance and mentioned that I was off work with depression, to which he replied, 'I wouldn't have thought that you were the type to be depressed.' This begs the question exactly what is the type? As I have since found out, depression is no respecter of persons: it has no social status, it does not care whether you are rich or poor and it can strike anyone at any time if there is a trigger. I was having a difficult time at work, but I was also faced with the fact that my eldest daughter was in her early teens, not quite ready to fly the nest, but certainly needing me less and less. In a sense, I was in the process of feeling abandoned by my children. Not that I knew that then, or that this would be one of the major causes of my depression – comprehending that would come a long way down the line.

The usual first-line treatment available for doctors dealing with a depressed patient was medication, generally antidepressants and sometimes with tranquillizers alongside if you were very anxious, as I was at times. The doctors pushed me from one approach to the next, so for quite a long time I tried many of the different types of antidepressants available, none of which really seemed to help much. I think some did give me some relief, but they all seemed to give me different side-effects, too, including encouraging me to eat more and thus gain weight. I have never been the skinny, worrying type of depressed person anyway, despite suffering from the aforementioned anxiety states and panic attacks at times, so generally comfort eating was the route for me. Yet I hated being fat and this led to one of the many vicious circles I found myself in over the years as my weight yo-yoed up and down.

By then I knew that antidepressants were very effective for a great many people – you could read many accounts where they had been an almost miracle cure – so I was really angry that they didn't work for me. I tried to follow all the rules and take all the medication diligently but on many occasions, while feeling better, I stopped taking it, only to then realize that, in fact, it had certainly been helping, even if it hadn't 'cured' the illness completely. At that time, I certainly did not realize that I had to help myself in order to get as well as I now am. This is some way ahead.

It would appear that my main problem at this time was that I couldn't find the answer I craved (an answer I believed would be the key to my recovery) to the question: why? Why me, why now? I had a loving, supportive (and very worried) husband and three lovely children with whom I had pretty good relationships. We had a nice home and plenty of friends; we didn't have money to throw around but neither did we go without. So I always came back to the question why?

Not long after I became depressed the strain on my marriage was beginning to tell and, although my husband and I visited a Relate counsellor for a few joint sessions in order to get help, I ended up going on my own. For quite a while I learned a lot about myself and made some steps forward, indeed it was that counsellor who suggested that I apply for a university course in order to prove to myself that I was still capable of study and betterment, although that caused problems of a different kind because my husband thought I would grow away from him. It did seem that as soon as one problem was solved, another reared its head, but I was trying to move forward and away from the depression that appeared to rule me.

I am certain that you have already come across most of the words used to describe depression – feeling blue, sad, unhappy, even desperate, to name but a few. What it is so difficult to do is to envisage just what those words actually mean to an individual who is depressed.

The words I use to describe my depression often relate to actions – running away; hiding under the duvet; being at the bottom of that deep, deep, pit; crying – and, sometimes, as I have added living out the actions that go with the words. But there was also, for me, a lack of colour, and a decrease of depth of feeling in all my senses; not that I literally felt blue or that I was under a black cloud, but that colour had been leached from my life. The flowers didn't look so beautiful, the sun didn't shine as brightly, the stars might just as well have not existed, even the leaves on the trees were simply green – they didn't have the range of different hues that I knew existed. Every single thing appeared monotonous, deadened, very much as I was. All of my senses were seriously affected, not only sight, but touch, smell, taste and hearing all suffered. I was unable to enthuse over a new song I had heard on the radio – in fact, very often the music would irritate me intensely. The sounds of people having fun, laughing, talking and enjoying themselves hurt my most innermost feelings because I was unable to join in, unable to be a part of normal everyday life any longer. No wonder I not only considered but attempted suicide. When you are dying from a major illness or accident, your body shuts down, sometimes slowly and painfully: that was almost what I felt was happening to me, but to my mind not to my body. My mind was becoming paralysed as a result of all the unpleasant thoughts that tormented me every minute of every day. I hated myself for all sorts of reasons and I didn't want to live with myself any longer. It almost felt as if an alien had taken over my mind and that I was at the mercy of forces I did not understand. It was very frightening.

I know I must have continued some form of life – eating, sleeping and so on – as, after all, I am still alive, but I know that I missed so many things because I was unable to take an interest. Sometimes, talking about holidays that our family took together when I was still very ill (life did still go on, you see), I find that I might have no recollection of something that we did, perhaps because my mind was too busy ruminating on some unpleasant thoughts.

The distressing feelings and thoughts that I was experiencing from the early 1990s were to continue off and on for a very long time, but in the meantime I hadn't been thrown on to the scrapheap completely by the medical profession, despite them finding me very difficult to treat. It appeared that talking therapies were the next string in the clinicians' bow. These had, of course, been around since the days of Freud but as a general treatment for depression were hard to come by twenty years ago and they were certainly not readily available on the NHS. However, as the various medications were apparently not having any real effect in shifting my stubborn and enduring depression I was referred to a psychotherapist. We got on very well and she told me that at first there would be lots of issues to consider but, as I got better, they would reduce in number until I had relatively little to say.

Strangely I can recall little of those sessions now, but I really did begin to feel a lot better, so much so that I went ahead with my application to study as a mature student at Loughborough. Happily I was accepted on to the course of my choice, immediately made three very good friends who were also mature students, and threw myself into the work. How I loved it – the challenges, the achievements! In the first two years I did not fail at anything, getting continuously pretty good marks for assignments until the time came for the second year exams, when I simply panicked. Looking back, I think I was probably frightened just in case I should fail; I ended up in hospital and seeing a psychiatrist for the first time. This wasn't good news for someone determined to succeed whatever the cost. I continued with my university essays in hospital, much to the amusement of the psychiatrist. When I asked for the tranquillizing medication to be reduced so that I could continue working, he said that he'd never actually had anyone under his care still trying to write essays while in hospital, and he wasn't sure what level of medication to put me on.

Around this time, through a quirk of fate or even divine intervention, call it what you will, I was lucky enough to become a patient of a clinical psychologist. My psychiatrist had referred me for group therapy and one of the psychiatric nurses who ran the group felt that I might suffer from SAD. She took me to see a psychologist who was interested in SAD, but he wasn't certain I suffered from the condition. However, he could see that I was 'a complete mess' (his words!) and took me on as a patient. I was now attending group therapy sessions and seeing both a psychiatrist, who mainly looked after the medication, and my new psychologist, with whom I had regular sessions. This psychologist was also a professor – not that his title made a positive impression on me at the time. In fact, his title caused me fear, anxiety and confusion at a time when I was already suffering from serious self-doubts, self-hatred and low self-esteem. I had recently been in contact with various professors at university and they were often rather scary individuals, very confident of their own position in life, which made the possibility of dealing with another academic somewhat terrifying. However, if all else fails – and it had – get in an expert, as they say. Although I did not know it at the time my new therapist was, even then, a leading authority in the world of depression, and he has been helping me to understand my illness off and on ever since then.

To begin with some of his techniques did seem strange to say the least. He would often draw simple diagrams of the brain in order to explain how the basic fight or flight system was part of the primitive brain and has remained within us even though it has little use in the twenty-first century. At the time I would wonder who was more mad – me or my therapist? It has taken me until now to recognize that, for me, flight was a major problem. I have already mentioned the fact that I would run away from my fiancé all those years ago. Then, during some of the worst times of my depression, I would run away in many different ways, physically, walking out, driving out in the car in the middle of the night, hiding under the duvet – all ways of trying to run away from thoughts that were just too horrible to *admit* to, even to myself. Now, of course, I can see the reasoning behind most of things we spoke about or acted on during the therapy sessions; back then,

I was frightened, confused, suicidal – basically I was that complete mess.

It has to be said that one of my difficulties, and I believe it is one that many people who suffer from depression encounter, was that I simply wanted someone to tell me what to do to get better – I would do it, I wouldn't be depressed anymore, and then I could get on with my life. Unfortunately that is just not feasible so it appeared that, with neither the medications nor the therapy working, I was doomed to depression for the foreseeable future. It is possible that, as you read this, you too can look back on therapy sessions where you blindly followed the lead of the therapist without having a clue where it was leading. I was struggling just to exist at this time; everything was just too confusing to be questioned. I worried about virtually everything I said or did and was in no position to begin querying the therapy sessions that were supposed to be helping me. Despite wanting a simple solution, take it from me, even when someone does tell you what to do to get better you either don't believe it or just cannot take it in – you simply want to put life into that 'too difficult box' and close the lid. However, I would urge you not do that: only with your positive help, even if all it amounts to is blind faith, can a therapist begin the long road towards your eventual recovery.

Many therapists use particular types of psychological disciplines and I even read some of the training manuals to see what was being used to try to help me. I hoped that if I could understand the techniques that my therapist was using I would be able to work with him more actively in order to speed up my recovery. It didn't work but it made for interesting reading. (Now, of course, we have the internet 'expert' at our fingertips, but it is best not to believe everything you read online, although there are some excellent self-help sites to be found.) Our therapy sessions were very much an exploration of ideas to see what might help. By this time I was firmly entrenched in the 'I'm never going to get better syndrome' and, when severely depressed, our brains simply do not work in a logical or sensible way. At times I'm certain that my therapist felt he was hitting his head against a brick wall as I consistently seemed unable to comprehend his very well thought out arguments and reasoning.

Each weekly therapy session left me feeling drained and sometimes even more confused. Before arriving I would tell myself that this week I would not cry, but sure enough at some time during every session I would burst into tears, apologizing profusely and using up box after box of tissues. One very good friend wondered why I continued going to the therapy sessions, saying that she was sure I was worse afterwards, yet I did persevere and, to my everlasting gratitude, so did my therapist!

Why so many tears? I honestly don't know. That they are a feature of depression is incontrovertible, or else why would every therapist's room I ever glanced into have a box of standard issue tissues on the desk? I suppose that one of the main features of depression is this terrible sadness that attacks you from the inside, even if the cause is usually initially unknown.

I was, however, improving. It was by no means a steady improvement – most of the time it was a case of one step forward and sometimes seven or even eight steps back –

but there did seem to be a light at the end of the tunnel, albeit a very, very long tunnel where the roof sometimes collapsed in a spectacular way, leaving me gasping under the weight of my fears, worries and anxieties. I could, and it seemed I sometimes did, worry for England. These worries covered every spectrum of my life, from the mundane concerns of whether the dinner would be over- or under-cooked, to my husband's late return from work having being caused by his death in an accident rather than the common fact that the roads were very busy. I do not understand where these worries originated; I have always liked things to be 'right' but not to the extent that they were now ruling my life in a very unpleasant way. It is horrible being so anxious all the time, and if you are suffering similarly you will know just what I mean; the anxiety seemed totally uncontrollable and would take over my whole thought processes so that it was very hard to function at all. It does still happen to me occasionally. It is very difficult to shift but I tell myself that it just me 'catastrophizing', as my therapist calls it – predicting the very worst possible outcome. I would see everything in black and white rather than in the various shades of grey that in reality exist in this life. And I would be overly concerned about silly things such as when I had a 'bad-hair-day', or felt fat and generally unattractive – in my mind these could amount to my being so unpleasant that other people just would not want to see me.

Right from the beginning my therapist thought that anger was behind my depression but this I could not and would not accept. I seldom lost my temper, my husband

and I did not row, and I have never thrown a plate at anyone!

It was decided that my anger, as I didn't even admit to it, must be severely repressed so once I was given a rolled up newspaper and told to hit a convenient chair with it, at the same time vocalizing my inner anger. Even in the midst of my depression I could hardly do this for laughing! All I could picture was how silly I must look. Although I had done amateur dramatics in my youth and certainly knew how to shout, this felt so false and I felt so stupid that it actually made me feel worse. I think we put that one down to experience and that perhaps we'd better try something else next time. It has actually taken me a long time to recognize when I am getting angry but I now realize that I definitely do get angry about all sorts of things. I have found that, once I recognize that there is anger, it is much easier to look at it dispassionately and then deal with it in whatever way seems most appropriate – not that it always works, as sometimes I get angrier just because I realize that I have become angry about something unimportant.

Hitting chairs in order to vent my anger sounds rather amusing and, looking back, it was, but I did try everything that was suggested during those difficult times: medications, anxiety classes, anger management classes, group therapy. I was desperate. I hated myself so much I tried to kill myself, yet so many people, particularly my family, but also many friends, seemed to like or even love me. How? Why? It didn't make sense to me. As far as I was concerned I was fat and ugly outside and fat and ugly inside. The reason I tried to commit suicide was that I thought that everyone would be better off without me because I was such a horrible being, not even nice enough to be called a person.

You hear of many celebrities being 'in therapy' as if it is just something you do if you are rich and famous but actually having therapy when you have severe depression is not an easy option. It is not a case of sitting in a comfortable chair or, as you might expect from watching American films, lying down on a couch whilst chatting with an understanding listener for as long as you like. In fact, I've never even seen a psychiatrist's couch even after all these years! If you are being treated under the NHS, as I was, don't even expect a comfortable chair. It is a talking therapy, but it is actually very painful and difficult to expose your innermost feelings to a stranger who, although they will have been trained not to be judgemental, may appear that way to you initially (when I felt much better I actually undertook a counselling course and gained some insights into the job of a counsellor). Another very difficult thing to accept is that this stranger will most probably understand the complex workings of your mind a great deal better than you do because they have been trained. This is frighteningly difficult to accept when you are very ill with depression. It is also very difficult to even begin to take on board the things that you might need to try and do to become whole again. If admitting that you are depressed is the first step to getting better then surely the second step is to learn to listen in a completely different way. I also needed to acknowledge many aspects of my basic nature that I had not considered before and that were in addition to my struggles with anger: that it is possible to fail as well as achieve and still be loved; that one the most basic human emotions is anger – it is within us all; that no person can possibly be 'good' all the time. I also had to understand that depression – particularly my type of depression – was often fed by my own bullying and negative thoughts. Also, when in therapy you not only have to want to get better, you also have to believe that you can, and that can be a very difficult, anxious and frightening process, putting yet more pressure on you when it might seem that you cannot face any more.

I was shocked when my therapist first suggested that I bullied myself. In my mind a bully said nasty things about you or was physically abusive, and it took a long time for me to see the truth behind my self-bullying. You could mistake your bullying for 'encouragement'. I certainly did: I encouraged myself to do better, to achieve more, to be more successful, to have my children better behaved than others. So here I had another set of feelings that were being challenged in no uncertain terms. Yet I clung on to all these feelings that were, at base, causing me so much distress, finding it so hard to see that I needed to change in order to get well.

How did I cope with simply living during all this time? How did I feel? I really struggle to find words to describe just how I felt at times – how, when things seemed to be looking up, I would suddenly be knocked sideways and return to those dreadful periods when I would believe I was useless, unnecessary, and would want to kill myself rather than continue with my futile life. I was so much better most of the time but there were still occasions when it seemed that all I could manage to do was to survive. I often felt that no one understood me – how could they when I didn't understand myself? I felt very alone and scared, almost like a child again, needing someone to run to for comfort and understanding, someone who would not judge me. I would often take the dog for a walk and find myself just sitting down in the field and crying and crying whilst the dog sat patiently by my side and licked the tears off my face. I still desperately wanted to be whole again; I wanted my husband to have his real wife back and my children to have their mum return to them, but I didn't know how to achieve that goal. At these times I couldn't see how anyone could say they loved me when I hated myself so much. Either I was right and I was hateful or they were right and I was loveable: I couldn't see that there was a huge abyss between those two concepts.

Having said all that, I was getting better, and this *is* a story of hope and encouragement. Amongst the setbacks, in 1996 I was eventually able to find a new job that I ended up staying in for eight years. I had understanding colleagues who became friends and who made the most of the highs (I was fantastic at clearing out the stockroom when I was high!), but also helped with the lows, and my immediate manager was fantastic. Most of the time I felt human again but, yes, I had bad times and once had to have three months off work as I struggled yet again; I re-entered the pit, my self-esteem hit rock bottom and I was convinced I was a complete failure. Feeling that I was beating this illness and then being knocked back was almost worse than being depressed all the time; you may find this difficult to believe but I can assure you that being in the land of no-hope can feel better than having some hope. It is very difficult to look your demons in the eye yet again and begin that terribly difficult struggle once more.

However, the general trend was up and I was much improved. I began to study for an Open University degree in 2000 and, as I was able to use credits built up from my studies at Loughborough, it took just a further two years to achieve my BA. I was so proud and I even had my picture in the local newspaper explaining that I had gained the degree despite being depressed during my studies. I had been very determined to complete it, whilst still finding it very difficult to admit that I might fail. I think I must have quite a lot of determination in my makeup –'If at first you don't succeed, try, try, again'. As I've said, I took on the pressures of the job and the degree whilst I was still depressed, although by now the hypomanic effect of being bipolar was also beginning to show itself properly. Of course, with hindsight I have probably always been bipolar. It has shown itself in various ways, mainly through always being busy and doing things – many of my friends have said that they would like some of my get-up-and-go, whilst I have retorted that I would like to stop and be able to do nothing! Whether I was depressed or hypomanic, I was still fighting to achieve, to be loveable and not to be abandoned, even if I still did not necessarily believe that this was the root cause of my problems.

Part of the therapy I was using then included the completion of 'thought forms' whereby I would note down something that had happened that had upset me, and then consider how it had made me feel, such as sad or angry. This would be followed by thinking of ways I could look at the event differently, trying to see my negative thinking for what it was. I would then look at the event from the point of view of a friend. It forced me to look at situations from another point of view other than my own, somewhat skewed one. Although I initially completed these forms for the benefit of my therapist, rather than for myself – almost as if it was homework I had to 'get right' – every form I completed was bringing me nearer to understanding my own negative outlook.

Eventually I did have to accept anger as the root cause of my depression, and it was only then that my recovery really speeded up. To do this I had to consider both the cause of my anger and its effect before I could begin to deal with it. People speak of the life of *Homo sapiens* as beginning right at the end of countless millennia after the formation of the earth; similarly, more than nine-tenths of the period of my depression was spent denying anger and only the last tenth accepting and dealing with it.

It may seem strange to be looking at the root cause of my depression at this late stage in my story, yet that is how it was. Perhaps if I had been able to accept this truth earlier I would not have suffered so badly. At times it was as if my therapist and I were speaking in different languages: he didn't understand mine and I didn't understand his, so this was quite a hurdle to overcome. Trust was another major issue. I have mentioned the difficulties involved in exposing your thoughts to a stranger and even after many years with the same therapist there were times when I was very angry with him (look, a breakthrough, I am admitting anger!) – that would lead to a return to that initial lack of trust. So we had to learn to communicate, to understand each other so that I could take on board what he was trying to explain in order to help me. I have said that my mind was often closed to his ideas, even blanking him out at times, but bear in mind that he was talking about emotions that I had never before acknowledged. Together we had to consider where the anger had come from, how it had grown and, finally how it had then turned inward so that it could bully me from within.

I had to admit that yes, I not only could but should be angry at times; that this was a normal, albeit primitive emotion that still fuels many people and societies today – or else why would there still be wars and murders? I was beginning to make huge strides now not only in understanding these basic emotions and acknowledging them but also in seeing how they impacted on me and how I needed to work with my anger, not deny it. However, it is impossible to try to change one's whole way of thinking without causing a lot of anxieties – perhaps this is why my recovery took such a long time.

Having acknowledged now that I did have anger in me, I felt frightened by it. You may remember that I had been unable to hit a chair with a newspaper but now the anger was acknowledged I was concerned at how forceful it might be. Would I now perhaps be capable of killing someone? I already hated myself and had tried to kill myself – would the escaped anger be so strong that I would now succeed in committing suicide? There were many questions, all unanswerable, yet my therapist did comfort me by reassuring me that he didn't consider me a psychopath!

I began this story by saying how difficult it now is to

remember the horrible times and yet they seem to be all I have written about. It is now time to redress the balance because, in fact, I feel so much better than I ever thought I could feel. So, what did make a difference? Firstly just dogged perseverance in so many ways: taking my medication even when I thought it wasn't doing any good; attending therapy sessions; reading self-help books to try to understand if it was possible to help myself; consciously wanting to get better and actively trying to get better; accepting that I had depression but that that did not make me a bad person and that depression was an illness. It might have appeared, reading my story up to this point, that during every therapy session some new, really serious problem reared its head but in reality it wasn't like that: I grew happier and more content. Yes, I still needed help but I was now even in a position to help other people with depression. Myself and a friend, who also had depression, set up a club for people to share their experiences, helping each other come to terms with the illness.

So bit by bit things did begin to improve. I was able to get out of bed in the morning and not hide away under the duvet; I stopped feeling suicidal and began to take notice of the world around me. I was able to smile at people again and they smiled back (as I got better my neighbour said to me that she had never been sure whether to talk to me or not). I took more care in my appearance but was less concerned with my body size as I became more comfortable with myself and within myself. I was able to show love to my husband and family again and even to accept that they did love me, warts and all. Yet there is one thing that I still struggle with from time to time, and that is to be kind, loving and compassionate *to myself*. Learning how to do that has been the biggest step in my recovery. It is impossible to quantify the thankfulness I feel that my family stuck by me through so many terribly difficult years, yet I do thank them from the bottom of my heart. My eldest daughter once said to me that when I was severely depressed and it was obvious that I was in so much pain she had almost wanted me to kill myself so that I would be at peace; of course, she hadn't really and was so glad that I didn't!

Many of the words I have used to describe my feelings are very familiar and are in everyday use. You read and hear about them on the news every day – words such as anger, shame, bullying, fear and hate – but they always seem to refer to other people, and not to us; yet those emotions exist in every one of us and, in the end, it was accepting that I too had those dreadful feelings inside me that really helped my recovery. As with all strong emotions we know that they need to be controlled but not denied. For many of those who suffer from depression the root cause will, I'm sure, be one of those emotions: the difficulty is facing up to that, recognizing it and then dealing with it. I still have issues with internal anger although I am better equipped to talk about it now, but my main difficulty is recognizing that this is what is driving either my depression or, more commonly now, hypomania, so I still have to pick up the phone and ask for help. But it's amazing how clear it suddenly becomes when, with timely advice and a closer look at what has triggered the feelings, I find that it's my old 'friend' anger again. Perhaps one day I will be able to recognize, analyse and deal with my own feelings just by myself – I'd better try as my therapist may retire one day! However, being able to ask for help is not demeaning: if you had a physical illness you might need a check-up at the doctor's or change of medication, so look on psychological advice as similar to physical help.

As I have said previously, my therapist is also a professor who researches the causes and treatments for depression, so he spends much of his time trying to understand just what makes someone with depression depressed and, having done that, formulating ways of helping those with this debilitating illness. The approach he used (and in fact developed) is called Compassion Focused Therapy and this had an incredible effect on me. It entails being kind and compassionate to oneself. Some of the members of the depression club helped out during the development and trials of this approach and, as one of them, I have to say that at first I treated this idea – to think in a kindly way about yourself – almost with derision (the actual words I used were that it was 'wishy washy'). Of course I was kind to myself, I thought, how could I not be? I was always kind and compassionate to other people and even to animals too. I really didn't have a clue what my therapist was trying to explain to me. Eventually I did realize, after a long time, that the crux of the matter was learning to listen to myself and learning how to recognize the feelings within myself, particularly those feelings of anger, of course. Then, and only then, could I begin to be compassionate to myself. This new concept seemed to be based on the 'thought forms' I have previously mentioned. However, in order to be compassionate to myself, what really helped me was to accept the insight as if it was coming from a friend; to help with this I imagine I have an alter ego – my compassionate self – and I have conversations with this other self in my head when something has happened that has caused me any kind of upset, be it anger, shame, sadness or so on. It doesn't come easily but you do need to practise being compassionate. This is still tremendously helpful for me.

I think trust is an important issue when dealing with both medication and therapeutic treatments for mental health issues. If your central heating broke down, you would call in an expert to tell you what the problem is. Usually, you believe them implicitly, trust in them and ask them to fix the problem: you don't often query their diagnosis. I found it much more difficult to have the same attitude to my depression, and many times I just did not believe what my therapist was telling me. You just have to feel sorry for these doctors and psychologists at times – how they stay sane when faced with such negativity is beyond my comprehension!

Luckily for us both, in recent times I have only needed a few words or occasional visits to help me get back on the straight and narrow after I have dipped into depression or a hypomanic state. My therapist's understanding of my convoluted thoughts and his ways of explaining where they may have originated helps me to appreciate what the driving force of the downturn might be. He helps me both understand the thoughts and cope with them, resulting in a tremendous reduction in their impact on my life so that I can function normally again in a very short time.

I am now staying with that most enduring label of

bipolar, taking my medication, listening to my emotions and trying to remember that when I begin to get depressed or very high it is more than likely my anger talking. I then need to meditate, to calm down, to be compassionate to myself and to take time to think of myself a bit more.

I now live a normal life, although eventually the pressure of holding down a responsible job became too much as I always tried to be everything to everybody – I was still searching for 'lovability' from colleagues, I guess, something that they were not in a position to give (I don't think that has ever been in anyone's job description!). I am, however, always very busy and that is not just when I am in a manic state! I easily fill my time with swimming, voluntary work, sewing and babysitting, and there is always plenty of that with six grandchildren. I also go to an art club once a week. My husband and I have a caravan and go away quite a lot in that now that he is also retired, and we walk and cycle (weather permitting). So life, on the whole, is fantastic. Yes, I still have issues with anger and recognizing that the driving force of my depression/ mania is anger, and I need to use my compassionate 'friend' to help me to put it into its place.

As I hope you can appreciate, throughout the years of my illness I have been helped in three main ways: with medication, therapy and self-help. It is fair to say that without all three tools I wouldn't be where I am today so I do still use all of them; the therapy has allowed me to understand the self-help techniques and, despite all that I have said about medication, I actually find it impossible to function without a mood stabilizer. However, therapy, by its very nature, is a finite resource but the self-help techniques I have learnt and still need to practise regularly will, I hope, prevent the illness returning.

One final point, very relevant to my particular circumstances, is that I traced my birth parents. I was able to visit my mother just a few short months before she died, although I had to go halfway round the world to meet her as she had emigrated to Australia in the 1960s. It was a wonderful experience. Although I have never met my father – coincidentally, he too lives abroad – we correspond regularly by email. I am certain that finding my roots has helped towards my recovery. Not only do I look just like my mother, my father also appears to have a degree of bipolarity in his nature, although he just calls it being very, very busy!

How I really want to end my story is to say that it is possible to recover from the deepest and most enduring depression. If, and it is a big 'if', you really grasp the nettle of wanting to get well and trying to get well, and do not expect there to be a magic pill that will cure you, then you too will recover, however long it may take. You cannot change your personality or what has passed but you can change the way you think about and react to what transpires in your life. For me, this means accepting my limitations and also that I may fail in some undertakings. I still find this incredibly difficult at times but I really am succeeding.

As the prayer of St Francis says:

Where there is despair, hope;
Where there is darkness, light;
Where there is sadness, joy.

I think that, perhaps, St Francis had suffered from depression sometime in his life, too, as he understood these feelings so well.

I have recently read a series of letters written by different celebrities to their sixteen-year-old selves and I thought that would be a good way to end my story. However, rather than a letter to my sixteen-year-old self, it is addressed to my pre-depressed self.

This is such a difficult letter to write, because at this time you may not believe anything that I am going to tell you. You will suffer greatly during the many years of your depression, so much so that you will think that life is not worth living and try to end your life more than once. Thankfully you will not succeed but at the time you will see it as the only course open to you. You will be bitterly ashamed of the hurt you inflict on your family, but what you perceive as your selfishness is only caused by the illness and this will seem particularly noticeable in someone, like you, who has previously been a happy, caring, loving and compassionate person. But, as the years pass you should take comfort from the love and support given to you by those most important people in your life. By succeeding in ending your life you would have missed so many things beyond compare, such as seeing the growth and development of your daughters into full and well-rounded people, followed by the opportunity to watch your grandchildren grow up, too. Looking back you will feel so honoured to be part of their lives, to have been both Mum and then Nana. So, as you suffer and are in distress of the most unimaginable kind during a severe and enduring depression, please hang on in there, it is certainly worth it. There are countless people who have suffered in a similar way and some of them will tell you that you will come out of this illness a better person, more understanding, more empathetic, more compassionate; you may not believe this now but it is the truth.

I am sending you all my love and strength and compassion to see you through the difficult times ahead; you see I know you can do it. This really will be a 'lifetime achievement' and so much better than any certificate or prize you could ever hope to get, even including that elusive degree you so hanker after.

All my love

Mary

5

Life after retirement

I am eighty-four years young, and I lived a very ordinary life until I retired at sixty years of age.

I am an ordinary working-class wee woman and although most of this story starts when I became sixty I would like to tell you a wee bit about how I got to retiring age and then how I coped with depression after I retired.

I was born in a town in the west of Scotland and still live there. I was the oldest of three children and had a poor but happy childhood in an ordinary home. We never had much but I was content, with a loving mother and grandmother. I loved school and did very well during my school years.

I left school and started work at fourteen, first of all in a chip shop and then with the local council.

At seventeen I went to the dance, like many of my friends, and I met my first husband there. I got married at nineteen and had my first child at twenty-one. Three-and-a-half years later I had another son. We were just a normal family but a few years later my husband became ill. By that time, at the age of thirty-one, I also had a wee daughter. By April that year my first husband died, when my daughter was only three months old. I was widowed for the first time at thirty-two, with three children.

Two years later I married for the second time and after another two years I had my youngest son. Over the years I worked between having my family, mostly in a chip shop at night when my husband was home. We were just an ordinary family and lived a normal family life.

At forty-eight I got the chance to take a course at a further education college in a nearby town. I learned to type, passed my O level in English with an A, had office training and was fortunate to take what was then called the 'Short Answer Test' to get into the Civil Service. I passed the test and was given a job with the Ministry of Defence. From the time I was young I had wanted to work in an office and at the age of forty-eight I realized my dream.

A year later my husband died very suddenly and once more I was left on my own with my family.

Over the years I had all the usual situations and problems relating to family life. It had been good and bad at times but there was nothing that I hadn't been able to cope with. I had, like many others, my share of sadness, happiness and love. I liked my job in the Civil Service and just got on with my life. By this time my two oldest sons were married and I had four grandchildren.

I made many friends, joined a social club and the years went by very quickly. My daughter was in the Women's Royal Navy Service and only my young son and I were left at home.

As I had worked most of my life I started to look forward to retiring. I had made up my mind that I would retire from my job by the time I was sixty. I went to pre-retirement courses through my work but in the end they were not what I needed. I decided that come hell or high water the day I became sixty would be my last working day. I had it in my mind that I would take a year off and then probably think about doing some voluntary work, but as events would later prove I made a very bad decision to wait a year before becoming involved in some kind of work. I retired on my birthday and I had a nice send off and lovely gifts from my workmates. I went on holiday to the Netherlands with my daughter for ten days, and then stayed with her at her home on the south coast of England, where I also visited my beloved sister and her husband. Then I came home to enjoy my retirement.

I retired at the end of March and after my short holiday I settled down to enjoy the summer. I had a great time and although I was living on less money it never worried me as I was used to living on a budget – it was part of my life. I went swimming in the local open-air pool, went on coach trips, joined an exercise class, walked a lot and really enjoyed all that lovely free time I had to do what I wanted. My younger son was still at home and I used to see him off to work at six o'clock in the morning and that was when my day started. As the autumn and winter approached I began to feel that something was wrong but I didn't know what. I began to find that all that lovely free time was now a burden to me and after my son went to work I began to feel lost.

When the summer finished, the coach trips stopped and our open-air swimming pool closed for the winter so I had nothing to fill all that empty time. I didn't know that this would affect me.

I didn't realize at that time that depression was starting to set in. It just crept up on me like a thief in the night and began to take over my life. As the dark nights drew in I started to have what I now know were panic attacks and I eventually got to the stage I dreaded going out. One day I got on the bus to the nearby town to get my shopping but when I arrived there I got off the bus, walked three or four yards and then turned back, got on the bus again and came home. I couldn't face or cope with things. My home became my refuge – I didn't want to go out and face people. I didn't want to answer the phone and I began to go down that long black tunnel of depression.

I was like that for some time and went to my doctor who gave me some tablets which were very mild antidepressants, which most of the time stayed in my bag and were never used. Although they helped my panic attacks when I took them, and helped me to get through the day, they were not a cure.

Many people speak about depression but only someone who has ever been there can really know how it feels to lose control of your life and how negative you can become. At that time every small thing set me off in a panic: it could be the telephone ringing or someone knocking at the door – just little things that became mountains to me in my mind; they were magnified and I just couldn't cope. I remember saying to myself 'stop the world I want to get off, I don't want to be here'. I was so negative. I also felt so ashamed of myself for all the stress I was causing my dear family. I remember one night being in my neighbours' house (we have been neighbours for fifty-six years) and just talking generally when I felt this awful feeling of panic for no particular reason and I thought, 'I don't want to be here.' I can't remember what excuse I made but all I wanted was to get back into my safe haven – my own house. Panic attacks don't always need something to trigger them off – they can just happen. You get this frightening feeling inside you and go to pieces. Everything became an effort. I didn't want to wash my face, comb my hair or do anything – it all became a burden to me just to try and be normal.

During that bad time my beloved only sister phoned me from England to tell me she had secondary cancer and only had a limited time to be here. That just really set me off; I wanted to see her but I was so far away. I got it into my head that I must go to her, but I wasn't in any state to make the journey and didn't have the fare. One of my dear friends, on seeing the state I was in, realized that nothing was going to stop me and she came to my door with the money for my fare, but she was so worried about me she took me to Glasgow and put me on the train herself. I don't know how I did it but something pushed me on and I got to see my dear sister. I spent the next fortnight with my brother-in-law, going to the hospital every day.

Sometimes when you are down you get an inner strength which helps you to cope.

That was a very sad time for me and I will never know to this day how I managed to get through it. It wasn't until I got the courage to ask my doctor for help that I made any progress. Every day was an effort – what I now call a non-day – because I was only existing. Of course, saying I couldn't cope all the time must have made my situation worse. As I became more depressed, I thought there was no light in my life.

This was just over twenty years ago. Back then, people talked about depression as if you had committed a crime. There were no support groups to my knowledge and the stigma and ignorance surrounding it was unbelievable. Now it is in the open, there are many support groups and it is high on the agenda of the Scottish Government. It is an illness that can attack all ages but it is hard to accept that someone who is older and has coped for all their years can have depression. I used to get angry with myself and feel guilty because of my age, but it is no disgrace, it can affect all ages.

My family helped me as much as they could but they felt helpless at seeing this woman, their mother who had always been there for them, reduced to a tearful wreck whose favourite expression at that time was 'I can't cope'. They couldn't believe that the person who had always been the rock of the family was now the one who needed help. My youngest son said at a later date that he thought I was having a nervous breakdown and feared I would be hospitalized. I was so lost and afraid of my own shadow.

Now, looking back, I would never like to go through that terrible time again and I think about the effect it had not only on me but on my family, but I am grateful today for their love and support when I was down that long, black tunnel.

At the beginning of the year I went back to my doctor. I was so lost and desperate that I cried in his surgery, asking for his help.

My doctor looked at this wreck in front of him and said 'I can tell you what to do but only you can do it.' He could see what I couldn't and he advised me to go out into the community and get involved in something and do it to the best of my ability. I realized later that my decision to take a year off had been a big mistake because I left myself with nothing to do and had no purpose to my life.

I went home in despair – how could I go out into the community and get involved when I didn't want to go out and couldn't cope with life? How dare he tell me, in my state, to get involved? I was so negative. I couldn't see that the doctor was right and that what he advised me to do was what I needed. I won't say what I called my doctor when I got home but over the next few days I kept thinking about what he had said and the more I thought about it the more I realized that there was no one to really help me so I decided to give it a go and try to do something for myself.

I won't pretend it was easy because it wasn't and I had such little faith in myself that I could not see a way forward.

I had never really thought about what I could get involved in, but after some thought I decided that maybe something like volunteering in a charity shop might be a way to start.

There were two mornings every week when I was especially bad and panicky: Monday and Saturday. I couldn't explain that feeling at the time but later I realized that on Monday morning I was always getting ready for my working week and Saturday was my shopping morning, but now, of course, I didn't have a job to go to and I could do my shopping anytime it suited me or I felt like it.

I went to a charity shop in the nearby town and asked for the manageress, who turned out to be a lovely lady. I told her my story and asked if she would take me on and give me shifts on Monday and Saturday mornings. The manageress listened and said she would give me a try and I could start the next week. That was my first real step on the road to recovery and I will always be grateful to her for allowing me to start working at the shop.

Of course no one knew I was a wreck because I managed to put on a brave face as I didn't want people to know how desperate and low I felt.

Writing about it now brings it all back but I am out of that dark tunnel and now I can cope with things.

The ladies at the charity shop were marvellous and even all these years later some of us still meet up in town and talk about the happy times we had in the shop. I owe a lot to the manageress and all the lovely ladies I worked with, many of whom are gone now, but they all helped me on my road to recovery.

There is no quick fix for depression and the problems it brings to your life but getting involved can sometimes help. Although I did not realize it at the time, I was in some ways already making progress. Even the thought of going to the charity shop was starting to make me feel better.

During that summer, when reading my local newspaper, an article caught my eye and my interest. The article was about a future conference in the local town hall which was being set up by the council with the idea of setting up a forum for the elderly in my local region. I phoned the number in the newspaper and said I'd be interested in going along and was lucky enough to then receive an invitation for the event. About 150 older people were there that day. There were speakers explaining what the elderly forums were all about and we were allowed to take part in workshops too. I was very impressed as I had never attended anything like it before and I got a good feeling about the day.

At the end of the afternoon they asked for anyone interested in joining a committee with the aim of setting up a forum in the local area to leave their name and address. Needless to say I thought this might just be something for me to get involved in and take me that step further away from my depression. Signing my name that day was another good decision for me.

After a few weeks the people who had put their names down were invited to a meeting in the nearby town to set up a committee. I attended that first meeting and ended up by being made Vice Chair by a complete stranger (in fact, they were all strangers to me). To begin with, I began to panic at the thought of being a Vice Chair but I consoled myself by saying a Vice Chair is only needed when the Chair is not there and I thought there was no danger of that. So I never said anything and let myself be nominated. For the first few meetings I found it difficult to cope with just being there. I was particularly stressed at the thought of going to meetings with complete strangers but as the meetings progressed we all got to know each other and I started to feel much more relaxed.

After about three or four meetings, the time came when I, as Vice Chair, had to take the meeting myself – on arriving at the meeting a gentleman told me that the Chair wasn't going to be able to attend as his wife was ill. I said, 'No way could I take any meeting,' but I was told that, as the Vice Chair, I *must* or else there would be no forum. He was quite adamant and put me in a spot. The last thing I needed then was to conduct this meeting. I was petrified at the thought of it, but I didn't want the forum to stop because we were all dedicated to really getting it going. So in spite of myself I took the Chair and managed to cope with great difficulty.

Little did I know that taking the Chair (or, as I say, being thrown in at the deep end!) that day would change my life for the better, forever. That day I took a step forward towards what has been an exciting and fulfilling adventure and, in fact, I am still the Chair after all this time!

It was the start of a long journey which is still continuing and I would like to tell you how it changed my life, and about some of the steps I have taken along this part of the road.

I stayed at the charity shop for about a couple of years but as I became more involved on committees representing older people, my diary gradually got filled up. But while I was still at the shop a book all about committees came in. I bought the book, took it home and read it until I had good idea about committees and the duties of the members. This was a great help to me as I really hadn't a clue even though I was now expected to know what I was doing and be in control.

Elderly forums are campaigning groups who take on issues of concern which affect the quality of life of the people we represent. This has given us a lot of pleasure and great fun especially when we are taking part in marches in all sorts of places.

We became part of an umbrella group of forums, and I served as the group's Vice Chair for two years and then became Chair for three years. Being Chair of this big group, which at that time represented seventy forums, gave me the experience and courage to speak up for others.

In my own forum we had a few years of hard work to let everyone know we meant business. I remember one instance when we had an issue about bad pavements and had been getting complaints about them from members of the public. We approached someone from the council's roads department who came to our committee, but he was very dismissive of us. We decided to do something to get him to listen, so we took pictures of bad pavements in many parts of the region and got petitions going. This gentleman, when he saw we meant business, included some of our suggestions in his next round of repairs. That was our first successful campaign and we were now up and running.

In the beginning we had support from the Social Work department of the council and had three workers who helped us on our way and gave us great support, but as our group progressed and money became scarcer we lost our support. By this time we were able to stand on our own two feet but we haven't forgotten how much we appreciated all the support and guidance we got from those people.

As we moved forward we began to be known and acknowledged for what we were. The next few years we worked on many different issues and people were asking, 'What is this group called an elderly forum?'

Although I am now classed as a public speaker I have never had any formal training to do this, but I had to learn on the job and that has been a really great revelation to me. I have spoken all over Britain and even in the Netherlands. My public speaking started when I was asked by a lady from the local Women's Guild if I would tell the organization what I was involved in. Public speaking hadn't come into my mind before and the very thought of it frightened the life out of me.

Eventually she persuaded me to give it a try and I agreed on condition that if I was not any good she would tell me and that would finish it. I went and spoke to about twenty lovely people who seemed to like what I said and no one threw tomatoes or eggs at me! I couldn't believe I had really done this and managed to pull it off.

Needless to say that was the start and it gave me the confidence to speak to other groups and at conferences. We all say we are never too old to learn and that is true, especially for me. When I started this journey I didn't know where I was going and had to learn all about pensioners' issues and be able to talk about them.

The good thing about being involved for some time is the connections you make along the way and the information you have about other groups. When Mrs Bloggs stops you in the street looking for answers to a question, even if you don't know the answer you can usually point her in the right direction. I began to realize that in helping others I was starting to help myself a bit further out of my depression. I began to feel good about myself and I realized that maybe I had something to contribute to society. By helping others and getting really involved I was becoming more confident and feeling happier with myself and my life; I realized that life was not over for me and I could still be of some use to someone.

As the forum progressed we were asked for representatives to sit on the committees of different groups, and guess who usually ended up by getting involved? Yes, little old me. I sit on about sixteen – five of which I chair – but I am happy to be involved because I know this is what I like and it keeps me going.

One public speaking event I particularly remember was on the terrace of the House of Commons. I was asked to represent Scotland at a meeting held by a national charity for the elderly. I travelled to London with another elderly forum representative and I was thrilled to bits to be taking part. We stayed overnight in a hotel and then were taken by taxi to the House of Commons. One of the highlights of that meeting, which was about transport, was meeting Robert Powell – it was such a lovely experience to meet one of my favourite actors and such a really nice man.

Another high-profile adventure was in Rotterdam, the Netherlands, in about 2004. I had been asked by representatives of a British-Dutch corporation to take part in a conference in London. I met some really nice people from many countries and really enjoyed the conference. A year later an email arrived asking me if I would be able to travel to the Netherlands – first-class, with all expenses paid – to take part in the corporation's annual conference. I was asked to speak as an elderly consumer. As I write all my own speeches and talks

I consulted my forum members for their ideas about issues for older consumers and also included my own experiences. I didn't know until I got there that there would be representatives from thirty-two countries present, but my talk went down really well. I was the only oldie there and I was treated like royalty. It was such a rewarding experience and such a worthwhile and happy time for me.

I feel very privileged and happy to be allowed to represent anyone. Sometimes I say to myself, 'Is this really me? How have I managed to get here?' I could go on forever about all the places where I have spoken, but I would like to tell you about just two other places that I have been lucky enough to visit.

The first is Number 10 Downing Street as one of a hundred older people who were the guests of Tony Blair and Cherie Blair. It was an evening reception during the Year of Older People. After the reception, my MP met me at the entrance to Number 10 and took me for dinner at the House of Commons dining room. The other memorable visit was to Windsor Castle during the Queen's eightieth birthday celebrations. The Queen officiated an awards ceremony which was very moving as the recipients were being rewarded for their charity work. Roger Moore, the film actor was one of them. There were loads of celebrities there and I met the newsreader Moira Stewart, who was the celebrity at our table. The lunch was excellent and very posh. It was a magic day and another unforgettable experience for me.

Quite recently someone said to me I don't know how you can be bothered with all these meetings, so I just said because I don't like the alternative. Many people don't realize just how much pleasure I get from being involved and to be doing something I like and every day is another challenge. It keeps my depression at bay. Over the years I have been involved in many groups and campaigns regarding the welfare of the elderly, including a group concerned with standards of care in residential and nursing homes in Scotland. I have been to many places carrying banners and placards, including protesting about pensions outside the House of Commons and about concessionary bus fares outside the old Scottish Executive building in Edinburgh. Once, in Blackpool during a pensioners' march, it was blowing a gale and pouring like mad with rain. The banner we were carrying got caught by a gust of wind and one of us virtually took off like Mary Poppins. We were drenched and sat all afternoon with our wet feet and soaked to the skin, but we were dedicated and determined to see it through. How is that for dedication – or were we daft? Happy times, indeed.

I must tell you now about some of the lovely surprises that have happened to me over the years. The local Rotary Club decided to give me an award for my work in the community. You can imagine how I felt – I couldn't believe that anyone thought I deserved an award and I thought they must have made a mistake. Incredibly more was to follow. In 2002, a national charity for the elderly presented me with a NOJO – Not Old Just Older – award at a star-studded event in London. To cap it all, about two months later I received a letter from Downing Street telling me I was being awarded an MBE by Her Majesty the Queen. No one can imagine how honoured I felt and

I still couldn't believe my luck. I had a wonderful day going to Buckingham Palace with my sons. By this time I had become a great-grandmother and now have eight great-grandchildren.

I continued to be involved with groups and committees that represent the elderly, including one created by a major charitable foundation in London. I was kept fully occupied with conferences, information days and with my other commitments – my family said they needed an appointment to see their mother. I was busy and I was happy but there was a shock waiting around the corner for me. Another incident in my life was going to upset my plans and start up my depression again.

On 7 January 2007 at 8.30 a.m. I started to feel unwell. It was a Sunday but my son eventually managed to get a doctor for me. He had me hospitalized right away and within twelve hours, thanks to a very brilliant surgeon, I was having a major emergency operation to fix a perforated bowel and had developed septicaemia. I won't go through all the details because I don't remember much about the next few days. I only remember this nice man telling me he had to operate. I can speak about it now because I am still here to tell the tale. I know that the man saved my life. I was in hospital for a fortnight and then transferred from the main regional hospital to a local unit set up for the assessment and rehabilitation of older people.

I will never forget the trauma of that time and how I felt or the care and kindness I received in both places, or the aftercare I got when I returned home. The shock of my illness was terrible – I was now a helpless person who was not allowed to open a door or do anything for myself. I had gone from an independent lady to someone who needed a lot of care.

The reason I am including this episode is because it had such a profound effect on my life. I had gone in the space of a day from someone who was out and about to what I thought was an invalid. When it all hit me it led me to think I would never be able to take up my life as it was. That was the second time depression hit me: I could hardly walk, had a zimmer and was so down in spirit that I just felt that my life was finished. When no one was around I used to sit and cry. I also knew that I was facing another major operation at the end of May and the thought frightened me to bits.

I started going down that long black tunnel again. During this time I felt so worried but never told anyone about my thoughts – they were kept for my down days. I got it into my head that I wasn't going to make it after my second operation. I thought I would be finished and that even if I made it I would never be able to get back to my groups. I felt so helpless and weak that I started to get negative about myself. I think now it was only natural and that many people in my situation would think and feel the same. However, I also realized I had been given a second chance and that I must try to pick up the threads and start being positive if not only for myself but for my family and friends, who were all there supporting me, and for all the medical staff who had got me through my operation.

I was not going to be allowed to go down that tunnel very far. My daughter stayed with me till my second operation and my friends informed me that

I was expected to be back in action again. As I gradually got a bit better the girls in the forum office decided that on a down day I was to take a taxi to the office and have a cup of tea and a chat with them. They were kindness itself: they helped my spirits and gave me the courage to go forward and not down.

I had cards and flowers galore and many visitors, not only in hospital but at home, and a steady stream of family and friends. I am so grateful for all the support from everyone and for the chance to get back to my community work. It took some time and I made many trips to the office for a wee laugh. I started to see that maybe, even if I wasn't as fit as before, I could still be involved.

After my second operation, it took some time to sink in but I could once again see the light at the end of the tunnel and I gradually began to take part in my meetings thanks to all the support and encouragement I received. This time I was not alone – all my community involvement had paid off for they were all there for me.

I didn't go back to London for three years and never thought in my wildest dreams that I would ever make it there again. However, I had a visit from the chairperson of the charitable foundation asking me to go back to London to rejoin the group. I knew that I was no longer able to travel that distance on my own but he said he would see what he could do. A member of the group, who has had a lot of experience helping the elderly, now travels down to London with me. No one can imagine the good feeling I had about being able to get to London again. I couldn't wish for a better companion than her and we have a good laugh together.

Near the end of 2007, as I was starting to get back on my feet, I was invited by the local Provost to a reception and received another award: this time I was the Older Person winner of the Provost's Equality award in the Health and Wellbeing category. I was highly delighted and very flattered to be given this very prestigious community award. It was another unexpected and very lovely gift out of the blue. Also, recently I was asked to become the region's Champion for Older People in the community. Sometimes I can't believe it but now I help to represent all the older people in the region. I've been lucky enough to appear on television several times to talk about fuel issues and other topics of concern to older people. I also recently appeared in an NHS video about depression in older people.

There are many situations in life which can make you depressed and sometimes issues can get you down but there is help out there and it is high on the agenda of the Scottish Government. Many older people are particularly depressed when they lose their partner after a long time together – sometimes the trauma leaves you lost and down. If you feel like that, go to your doctor and ask for his help. There is no disgrace in feeling depressed.

I was fortunate that my doctor could see what my problem was. The same sort of problem can come about after an illness or something stressful such as moving house, and sometimes a family problem might have arisen to make us weighed down with worry. As I said before, my retirement started me off and I always say to anyone nearing retirement to put something in place to be involved in.

Although there is still a lot of ignorance and stigma attached to what they now call mental health problems, including depression, there are many groups and professionals trying to make a difference to our lives. I am involved in one group involved in the mental health of older people in Scotland, but there are many other groups covering all ages because we all know that depression doesn't care about age and many younger people are also affected. You can't put a bandage or plaster on depression. I call it the silent illness because it sneaks up on you.

One of my friends recently asked me if I could tell her when my depression ended. I can honestly say I didn't wake up one day and say, 'Oh great, I am not depressed.' It took a few years and only as I became more involved in the community did my depression sneak away. I still can't say when, but I am so glad and happy that it finally disappeared. Now I have my good days and bad days like everyone else – it is part of living. Sometimes when I look back I say to myself, 'Did all that dreadful depression really happen to me? Was I that lost soul?' But I believe that you learn something from every situation in your life and that things happen to you for a reason. I reached out to the community and it helped me. If I feel down now, as everyone does at times, I go up to the office or I go out to the shops. If it is at night I lift up the phone and call my family or friends. I hope that anyone in that situation would be able to reach out to somebody – just knowing that you are not alone and that someone wants to listen can help you to cope. It is that feeling of isolation and helplessness that can take hold of you sometimes and we need to feel wanted and the sense of belonging. One of the things I have learned is to be able to put myself in the shoes of other people suffering from depression. When I meet someone who tells me they have depression, I can take my mind back to those terrible days and can genuinely feel for that person. I am not just paying them lip service: I can really relate to how they may be feeling. Try and get involved in something – it doesn't matter what; we all need an interest of some kind. It could be joining a group, volunteering in a charity shop or any kind of project.

I never thought I would see the light at the end of that long, black tunnel but I came out and I can understand how this illness can affect you and your family. I now have what I call my new career and will keep on as long as I can. Every day is a bonus and I look forward to whatever fate sends me. I wait for the next challenge.

THERE IS LIFE AFTER DEPRESSION, even if you can't see it. My wish would be for everyone with depression to someday get their life back and come out of that long, black tunnel.

As for me, I am as happy as Larry. I am still travelling along the journey and who knows where it will take me.

6

It's been a long time coming

I never envisaged being where I am today, leading a normal life, working in a job I love, being with my husband for twenty years, settled in our flat for nearly the same length of time and enjoying hobbies and interests that give me a lot of pleasure.

Back when I was a teenage girl, moving schools from England to Scotland was meant to have made a difference. I thought it was the answer; I was convinced that by staying where I was I would continue to be in a very dark and sinister place in my head. Being sixteen, I didn't have any idea about depression: all I knew was that I was miserable and that moving school surely was going to bring about a really positive change and a chance to get on with my life and be a teenager. Within eight weeks I was lying in A&E completely confused and disheartened that nothing had changed at all.

I'd not had the best start in life but that wasn't due to poverty, health or social issues – it was just due to the fact that my parents were really bad at relationships! It turned out that this single factor and its knock-on effects would have a very big impact on how I developed mentally and emotionally. The exact details of my early beginnings are a little sketchy because I have been given different accounts by various people who were around at the time. This, I think, is purely due to individual interpretations, assumptions and opinions, but it means that I'll never know the full answers to some of my questions about the past.

My dad had already had one marriage behind him when he married my mum. She was emotionally very immature (so various people have said) and really didn't want to settle down and certainly didn't want children. Within a few months of my birth, my mum had run away, frustrated with being tied down looking after a baby. She came back, only to run off again several times. It wasn't long before their relationship broke down for good, and my dad was granted temporary custody of me. While legal teams were organizing the case for permanent custody, my dad accepted a temporary job in Spain and took me with him. While there, he met my stepmother, who had two boys, and we all returned to live in England. Relations between my mum and dad continued to be very difficult and disruptive – on several occasions she refused to return me after custody visits, so the police would have to fetch me. Over the years she became increasingly unpredictable, saying she was going arrange things such as holidays and then letting me down. Over time this messed with my head: I started to distrust her intentions and feel she didn't really care.

As I got older, home life also became increasingly stressful. Unfortunately, my dad's relationship with my stepmum wasn't really that good and my relationship with her was even worse. In fact we spoke very little and

I felt very frightened of this woman who had become part of my family. I got on quite well with my stepbrothers, but all in all we were a very divided family: my dad and me on one side and my stepmum and her sons on the other. Arguments between my dad and stepmum would sometimes become violent and could go on for hours. I suffered psychological abuse and occasional physical abuse from my stepmum, while my dad became very distant, preferring to spend long hours away from home to avoid the arguments and fights. When it became time for me to go to secondary school, my dad asked me if I'd like to go away to boarding school. Having read the whole series of Enid Blyton's books set in St Clare's and Malory Towers, I agreed, but my decision was definitely based on fiction rather than fact! I also felt the need to get away from all the stress at home.

I struggled at school in all ways – emotionally, academically and because I was disinterested. I did have good friendships though, and they gave me a much needed distraction because by the time I was fourteen my mental well-being was deteriorating. I couldn't stand being in my own head. I often struggled with sleep and I felt tearful, hopeless, empty, desperate and confused. I wasn't able to put my head down and study, and my dad's relationship with my stepmum had broken down completely. One weekend I went home to collect some of my belongings, put them in the boot of my dad's car and my dad and I left everything else behind.

I felt immense relief that it was now just the two of us, albeit for a very short time, but in terms of my emotional welfare the damage had already been done. It didn't help my confusion that my dad had met someone before leaving my stepmum and she quickly moved in with us. I continued to struggle at school, with my reports including words and phrases like 'doldrums', 'lack of interest', 'not bothered', 'not paying enough attention' and 'needs to do a lot better'. They also said that I was more than capable if only I worked harder. Looking back, the school didn't know how I felt, so the reports are understandable.

In the Easter holidays before my O-level exams I went away to a revision study course to try and improve my chances of passing my exams. The set-up there was really good, but once again I was on a self-destruct mission and myself and others spent many evenings getting drunk and staying out until all hours. Two nights before I was due to come home, we were having a leaving 'do' and going round some pubs. Once again I got hopelessly drunk, ended up on a date and was then raped. I came back to my accommodation and spent five hours in the shower, but told myself it was all my fault, that I brought it upon myself and that I should have known better. I was never fully to address this issue until many years later.

When it came to taking my exams, I just wanted to get them out of the way and pushed my dad to let me leave school when I'd finished. He wanted me to stay on at the same school to take A levels but I somehow managed to convince him to let me move to a boarding school in Scotland, as all I wanted to do was get away. I also thought this change would bring about a whole 'new' me! If I'd not been carrying round all this 'baggage' it would have worked out well, but instead I arrived at my new school and promptly fell flat on my face. I tried to convince myself that I was having a great time when deep inside I felt awful and disappointed with myself. I felt so empty. The sad thing is that it was a really pleasant, friendly and supportive school, but my emotional needs couldn't be met, although they did try! Two months after I'd arrived, one Saturday I stayed overnight at my mum's (she had stayed in Scotland ever since leaving my dad). I went out in the evening with friends and on Sunday I woke up and felt like the world didn't need me in it. What was I here for anyway? What was the point?

While my mother was out, I sat in silence for the whole afternoon, contemplating what to do. I then went to her bathroom cabinet, grabbed all the pills I could and took every one of them. I had no idea what I had taken, but part of me was very scared as I started to feel very unwell. After an hour I panicked and called an ambulance. After that is a blur. My mum arrived at the same time as the ambulance and I was taken to hospital where I had my stomach pumped and was treated for the overdose. In the morning I was assessed by a duty psychiatrist. Meanwhile, my dad had arrived from England. I felt very ashamed and scared, and having my family there, knowing what I'd done, only made these feelings in me more powerful. All along the journey of my depression they've always said 'you should have spoken to us', but with family that's easier said than done. To this day I am a great believer in accessing professional, outside help and support so that feelings of guilt, shame and embarrassment can be avoided. Also, there are some things you want to talk about in a confidential and private environment without judgement. I didn't realize this at the time and therefore I questioned myself over and over as to why I couldn't talk to anyone in my family.

After a week I went back to school on the basis that I would promise that I would speak to someone if I felt that way again. By this time it was November and I had only been at the school for two months. I saw the duty psychiatrist every six weeks to monitor how things were going. He felt there had been a big build up to what had happened and that my family should be the ones to help me through it. With hindsight – what a great thing! – I can see that this was never going to work. So, I continued to struggle and started writing a diary to try and help me organize my thoughts and empty my head. Just after my Higher prelims in January I packed my things together at the boarding house and moved in with my cousin who worked shifts, with the idea being that when my Highers were finished I'd officially leave school, live there and find work. I felt relieved that I'd be staying in Scotland and hoped that things would improve. I went between the flat and school, but by March I was just aimlessly trying to get through each day in what felt like a haze of fog.

No matter how hard I tried, I found it impossible to broach the subject of how I was feeling with my family and even my friends. As a teenager communication is difficult enough as it is, but I was incapable of expressing myself with so many doubts, worries, concerns and anxieties about doing so. I felt that no one would understand how I was feeling, that they would brush it off as teenage problems and make judgements about me. I also felt pressure on me to do well in life as all my family were living successful, happy lives. I managed on a few occasions to phone the Samaritans as I was at my worst at night-time, having spent all day covering up my emotions. I then felt guilty that I didn't feel any better having used this means of support and this only confirmed in my mind that there was no hope.

By April I decided once again that I'd had enough, but this time there was a difference. Last time I had reacted impulsively to how I felt; this time I planned many days in advance, writing a note and meticulously thinking everything through. However, on the morning of my planned date, I received a letter from an interview I had attended for a job. I had been offered the job! I spent the next two hours in turmoil, racked with guilt, pacing in my room, knowing that there was no way I could take the job! I could barely get out of bed, look after myself and be with other people, never mind work! I felt completely useless and there was absolutely no way back.

I went ahead with my plan that evening and unfortunately my poor cousin was to be the person who had to phone for an ambulance when she came home from her shift. This time my family expressed much more emphasis on their belief that what I had done was unacceptable and not fair to everyone around me. While I was in A&E, I wondered what was going to happen next – discussions, meetings and so on were going on in the background. I had another psychiatric assessment and it was felt best that I should be admitted to a psychiatric hospital for a more thorough assessment. I was seventeen and spent the next six weeks on an adult psychiatric ward. More meetings and talks occurred between my family and the professionals taking care of me, and as a result I then had a visit from the nursing staff from a young people's unit who wanted to offer me a place for intense therapy, support and treatment. I didn't want to go back to the flat and I had felt no better having been on the psychiatric ward, so I accepted.

Before this point the belief was that my feelings were just 'teenage angst' and that over time I'd adjust and come through it. After arriving at the unit, the term 'depression' was mentioned and, after some more psychological assessments and questionnaires, I was told I had clinical depression and most likely had done so for around two years. In many ways it was a relief because at least I felt I had a diagnosis that I could work with and also I could explain to people that what I was feeling was valid. However, as I was still feeling so unwell, the diagnosis also made me wonder what my future would entail.

As I was later to find out, it is hard to come by a place at an adolescent mental health unit. Although as a group of teenagers with all different kinds of mental health issues we were rebellious, and at times resistant to being helped and supported, the structure was important. I was allocated a key nurse, with whom I would have support sessions, saw a psychologist and psychiatrist on a regular basis, had group therapy, family therapy, psychodrama and group meetings. Because of the range and level of therapies, we were all there for quite a while. I also had my first experience of antidepressant medication, which made a big difference to my ability to motivate myself and take part in the activities that were offered. After six months I was ready to be discharged. I went back to stay at my flat with my cousin and had weekly outpatient support sessions at the unit. I had made some good friendships at the unit and, after a couple of months, myself and another girl who was treated there decided we wanted to share a flat together. It also meant I could distance myself more from my family who I felt still didn't fully understand what it meant to have depression. It would have been easier for them to connect with something physical that can be seen, treated and cured. My family are not ones for talking about feelings and emotions, but this is what I needed, so I felt very different from them. By putting some distance between us it made it easier for me to talk and share things with others in similar circumstances.

At this time, I still didn't know what future I had or what I wanted to do with my life. I had been in hospital during the time I was due to sit my Higher exams and so the final results went on my prelims, which meant that I only passed one Higher (in Art). A lot of time, money and effort had been spent on my education, so I felt a great deal of guilt within me, knowing that it had amounted to nothing and that I had no real direction. However, my godparents gave me a job working part-time in their shop, with the idea to bring about routine and stability – something which had been lacking for such a big part of my life so far. By now my dad was on his fourth marriage and my mum had been married three times. I'd moved around so much between them and being at boarding school that I'd never really stayed in the one place for very long.

Over the next year I continued to struggle, but I was above water and tried as best as I could to move on with my life. I went on from working in a shop to attending an

IT training programme for people with mental health issues, which gave me some really good skills that I have used ever since. At times it was difficult to stick to a regular routine. I found it hard to get up at a set time every morning because my sleep was regularly disturbed; my depression was also very different on a daily basis – some days were better than others which meant on I could achieve more. There were times when I was off sick and unable to attend my weekly outpatient therapy sessions at the unit, but despite this I kept up with them and had regular medication reviews. Sharing a flat with my new friend didn't work out as well as we hoped as she too had spells of being unwell and in hospital. The situation ended up being a counter-productive one for us, instead of supportive.

Just after my nineteenth birthday things started to go downhill again and active thoughts of suicide and self-harm reared their ugly head. What was extremely hard for me was that I had been given so much external support since I had first been in hospital at age sixteen that guilt was to play an even bigger part in destroying everything I had struggled to achieve since then. For the first time I also experienced new symptoms of fear, paranoia and voices telling me that I was a really bad person. Looking back, I think the guilt played a big part in altering my thought processes and in creating more confusion. This was still seen as part of my depression, but a different approach to this needed to be taken, so reluctantly I agreed to another admission to the unit for assessment and further treatment. This time I stayed as an inpatient for five months.

It was slightly easier in that I knew the routine, but because I had been independent I found the restrictions difficult. I also was very fearful of talking about how I was feeling and what was going on inside me because I was so paranoid. I thought the staff hated me and were talking about me, and that anything I would say to them would be laughed at. While I was there I decided that when I was well enough to leave I wouldn't return to my flat and I applied for a supported accommodation place, sharing a small house with others in a similar position. I went through some medication changes and gradually, with the help of psychotherapy, art therapy and group therapy, started to feel a bit better. After a break of a few months, I returned to the IT programme and gained more skills and knowledge in computing and technology. Looking back I don't think I really appreciated what I'd achieved and didn't see it as very much apart from passing the time. I knew at some point that my time at the training programme would come to an end. I had already been there a total of eighteen months, but I hoped that with a new start in my new accommodation I could finally get a break.

I settled in to my new surroundings and got to know my fellow housemates, who all had different mental health issues including depression, self-harm, eating disorders and psychotic disorders. It was there that I met my future husband, which was completely unintentional and unplanned as I was still trying to sort myself out. It was one of those fluke situations whereby we just clicked so well: we chatted, laughed, watched films together, played pool and went for walks. Soon we went on picnics, then daytrips and even took a short break.

Everyone around us was sceptical, unsure and uncon-
vinced that this could ever work out, especially as I was
still experiencing significant difficulties with my depression. People wondered how on earth I would be able to
cope with a relationship, especially if it was to break up!
Nevertheless, just three months after I'd moved into the
house we bought two engagement rings and soon became
officially engaged. We came across quite a bit of resistance
and bewilderment, mostly from family members, at what
we were doing. Even staff at the young people's unit,
which I was still attending for therapy once a week, said
that they felt that this was not the right time to be getting
into a relationship but they said they would be there for
me if it didn't work out. It was then that my fiancé bought
me a budgie that was to become our beloved companion
and widen our interest in pets and animals.

After only nine months of being in supported accommodation, we were offered a one-bedroom flat in a nice
quiet area. It was summertime and although the move
was hard work and stressful, we settled ourselves in along
with our new budgie. We were on benefits so income was
tight and I still wasn't sure what I was going to do. I had
learned many new skills on the training programme, but
still didn't know how on earth I was going to apply them
in the real world. My fiancé was doing a training-for-work
scheme with a wildlife trust so was out early in the
morning and wasn't back until teatime. This meant that I
was by myself for a good part of the time and inevitably I
could withdraw into myself at any time and become
increasingly unwell. I was very unmotivated, lethargic
and flat, and on many days I didn't get up until lunchtime.

The staff at the unit suggested I attend the day centre twice a week for activities and company, and also to keep an eye on my mood fluctuations and mental health. I did enjoy the day centre and not long after I had started I had a review with one of the psychiatrists who suggested I try a new medication that may help with the more troublesome symptoms of my depression – the lethargy and lack of motivation. Within six weeks of being on the new medication I emerged with much more energy, zest and a spring in my step. I still had a long way to go, but this was the first time that I felt some hope that I would be able to recover from depression.

A downside remained, though: I still somehow didn't feel a worthwhile person. I had a mountain to climb in how I saw myself and my abilities. I was also still relatively young and, even though my fiancé was seven years older, we did silly things that jeopardized my recovery. One of those was binge drinking – this brought out demons from my past and I often ended up in very dark places in my head. I still had not fully worked through what had happened to me at sixteen when I had got drunk and left myself vulnerable. I also continued to have a very difficult relationship with my dad as I felt like I was this very small child, answerable to his every opinion, thought and views. In fact I had yet to develop my own identity. I also had zero assertion skills and could never stick up for myself, much to my fiancé's annoyance!

After a particularly heaving drinking session, I took an overdose of a very sedating medication. My initial intention was to do myself harm, but in reality it was a temporary suicidal thought – the sort I often had but didn't act on. I went straight to bed, without my fiancé realizing what I'd done, and fell asleep. In the morning he got up and left me lying in, thinking that obviously I needed to sleep off a hangover. By lunchtime I still had not got up and, when he couldn't wake me up, he realized that something wasn't right. Although he was very aware of my depression, this was my fiancé's first experience of my direct self-destruction and he was very upset. He called the emergency services and I was taken to hospital to be treated for my overdose. As I was still having treatment at the young people's unit, they continued to provide outpatient support.

Over the next few years we settled into a routine: my fiancé did odd jobs here and there and I continued to attend various support groups and therapies, along with having medication adjustments, all in the hope that one day I too would be able to work or do something mean-ingful. We got married in 1995 – just ourselves, the registrar and a couple of witnesses in a small village. We were very much connected with each other and as the years went on it became obvious that our relationship was going to work despite all the obstacles. We also have a great love of animals and, along with our budgie, we kept fishes and as a hobby I bred birds and chinchillas. As I spent a large amount of time in the flat, there was little doubt that not only did I learn a lot from this hobby, but it gave me a routine that I enjoyed immensely. At times I was in hospital so it was left to my fiancé to look after the animals, so it was a good job he had the same passion! Although we have had to reduce what we keep, we would never be without a budgie, and our current one gives us immense pleasure and fun. The companionship of keeping pets in helping depression can never be under-estimated – they're always there for you and never judge!

There was one last traumatic event that was really going to test our relationship and also test whether I would ever leave this awful depression and everything that went with it. I had a period of stability, not to the point of being able to work, but at least there was some 'calm'. This all came down with a crash when I attended a review at my local day hospital and started a different type of medication. It turned out that I had a paradoxical reaction to it and as a result began to feel extremely unwell, not only mentally, but physically. Within a matter of months I once again tried to take my own life. I spent several weeks in a psychiatric hospital over Christmas and upon discharge went into a space in my head I had never been to before. I can only describe it as is utter despair and anguish, and the need to escape became ever greater. I ran away to another city. I felt that if I was going to take my life it had to be somewhere I wouldn't be found by people who knew me, where it wouldn't be as upsetting, and creating that distance would be easier for me to complete it.

I couldn't have been more wrong in all aspects. The anguish and despair I put my husband and family through was immense. I was reported as a missing person and caused deep heartache back home. I was, of course, going through my own torture and, after two days and failed attempts on my life, I phoned the Samaritans who encouraged me to call the police. This I did and that evening I was taken into custody and then transferred to hospital for treatment. My husband held my hand for hours afterwards trying to reassure me that nothing mattered in life except us and that I was worth fighting for. I felt I didn't deserve his understanding and patience with me. I felt I had already put him through so much and that I would end up breaking him too. I was fragile, but so was he because he always had to hold everything together and to me this wasn't fair and wasn't how I wanted our relationship to be. If this continued for too much longer something was going to break.

Over the next few weeks in hospital I was offered electroconvulsive therapy, but decided to try a new medication instead. This took a while to take effect, so I didn't come home for three months and my husband was doing his best to work, look after the flat and visit me nearly every day. It was a good job we'd both decided early on in our relationship not to have children as he'd have had all that to cope with too! There is no doubt that my husband's health suffered and he had to attend our GP for stress-related problems. Upon my discharge a more substantial support package was put in place. I attended my local day hospital three days a week, where I took part in activities; I was allocated a key nurse to talk to once a week; and I was able to chat to others who were going through similar experiences. Even so, I had a few more hospital admissions over the next couple of years.

In 1997, we decided to venture into buying a computer. As I had been trained in IT skills I had never used, my husband thought that this would be a big help to me and I could also teach him. We connected up to the internet and I found a whole new world, albeit still very small at this point. I found sharing the thoughts and feelings related to my depression very useful and supportive, so much so that I set up my own website and over time it became a useful, supportive, interactive community. I see this particular venture as a pivotal moment for me and one that gives me immense satisfaction and a feeling of achievement, as it is something I continue to be involved in to this day. Nowadays there are many more sites that provide support and help, which is great.

In 2000, I had what turned out to be my last admission, although I didn't know it at the time. By then I'd had a history of depression going back thirteen years, but I was still with my husband and was even more determined that my problems had to change. This was the start of a long slow journey to recovery and one that I am extremely proud of, bearing in mind where I am today. I became better engaged with the activities at the day hospital and attended more regularly. Part of the reason for this was that, due to medication, my mood was more stable and I was able to stick to a better routine as a result. The next stage for me was to apply for help from a support worker from a mental health organization that offered a range of services that helped people to maintain their independence in the community. This would take me away from the very clinical, medical environments I'd been part of for so long. I wasn't really sure what support workers did, but initially I was offered a couple of two-hour visits. My support worker would visit me at home, where we spent some time getting to know each other, going for walks, having a cuppa and improving my social and communication skills.

It was at this point that, as a result of a leaflet coming through the post, I discovered what the Open University had to offer. Before, I would always ignore these things but, because my interest in life was returning, it appealed to my curiosity. I checked the Open University site online and was amazed at the vast range of courses. The style of open learning meant that I could be flexible with my studies, i.e. doing work/assignments when I felt OK and being able to take breaks when I didn't. It also meant I could study from home using my computer and didn't have to attend classes, and this helped a great deal in the early stages when I was still building my confidence and self-esteem. I initially signed up for an IT Certificate with a view to seeing how it went and if it didn't work out then I wasn't committed to continuing if I didn't want to. I was able to chat to my support worker about how I was getting on and any emotional concerns I had. I also started to go swimming with my support worker and then one day she suggested we try the gym. Over the years, due to lack of exercise and various medications, I had put on an enormous amount of weight. This definitely didn't help my confidence and self-esteem. So I felt I had nothing to lose, but did worry about my ability to sustain going to the gym as it felt such a big mountain to climb.

Between my Open University studies and going to the gym with my support worker things were looking up: little things were changing; I was starting to feel more positive; my confidence was growing; and I had more 'up' days than down. I loved the Open University courses so much that before I'd completed my first IT Certificate, I had already signed up for another course. The flexibility and being able to study at home suited me well. I also found that I was an extremely self-motivated person and had no trouble with assignment deadlines. As I had never been particularly suited to taking exams, I relished and enjoyed writing assignments much more as I was able to give so much more time to them.

After attending the gym for six months and increasing the level of exercise, I was becoming stronger. I had lost nearly two stones and was really starting to feel positive and hopeful. With that came back all the ability, skills, emotions, feelings, determination, maturity and humour that had been tucked away for so long. My husband told me recently that he felt they were always there – it was just that the depression controlled them. Now I was starting to take control. Managing long-term depression is hard work, but if you can keep some control then you can always be one step ahead of it. I also felt for the first time that I had a brain and I was now making use of it. In a very small way this made me a little sad, but only because I had really missed out on so much for so long due to my depression. I remember someone saying, 'Don't regret what you've done, regret what you've not done', and in many ways I had a lot of catching up to do. This only made me more determined to never again be in that place where I had no control and was taken over by depression.

The sessions with my support worker were reduced to once a week and we kept the focus on exercise, but I still had someone to bounce worries off and who would support me with any blips. I started attending the gym for an additional two days a week by myself and my weight loss continued.

By 2004 I had completed two years with the Open University and decided to start a course in Health & Social Care as I had an idea about trying to get involved in voluntary work in the social care sector. My sessions with my support worker came to an end: we'd come to a mutual agreement several months earlier that I was ready to move on and that the aims of the service – to regain my independence – had been achieved. My confidence was getting better by the day and I still had the help of my husband, my biggest supporter in my recovery. My relationship with my dad and family was also very different. I was starting to be 'me' and now I felt I could be assertive about my opinions and views. I had much less fear about being challenged by people. I am a naturally passive and patient person, but in the past I used to be very scared of people's anger and confrontational differences, and felt that my opinion about anything was worth nothing. This was not a healthy passiveness – it made me meek and meant that people could easily take advantage. I was able to retain my passive nature, but in a much more controlled way that meant I still had a voice. It's hard to know exactly the reasons for this change, but I think that being older and more mature, while feeling better and having my depression under control, had an overall positive impact.

The Health & Social Care course made me start to think about how I could help others. If I continued my own recovery I could use my own experiences to give help to those who continued to struggle and also support some of the services that had helped me. I was still attending a local drop-in centre twice a week and had been part of their committee, initially as a member and then as Secretary, and had learnt a lot about how services and organizations are run. I also used the skills that I had retained from my IT training way back in the late 1980s. We regularly hosted talks and visits from other services promoting what they do and how they can help and support people.

We had a visit from a mental health advocacy organization and in some of the material we were given there was a very big focus on using volunteer advocates. Full, intensive training was provided, along with continued support and development. I applied to take part in the advocacy organization's next course and within three months was making tentative steps at providing advocacy. Being an advocate entailed assisting service users to express their thoughts and preferences about their own mental health needs and about other issues which affected their lives. This included listening and helping people explore options, attending meetings and appointments, helping draft letters, accessing information and offering moral support. As my confidence continued to grow, I started to work with a wide range of issues and problems that crop up for anyone who has experienced mental health difficulties. This involved housing, benefits, attending medical appointments, childcare, complaints and representation.

By the following year I had completed my Health & Social Care course and felt I had gained an enormous amount from my voluntary work. It also meant something useful on my CV which was extremely blank and non-descriptive. I was starting to think about my options regarding work – by now my psychiatry appointments had been reduced to once a year and my medication was working well and keeping me stable – but as I was still on benefits I needed to find out how I was going to return to work gradually while still staying on the right side of the law. I was able to get in contact with an organization that provided a Disability Employment Advisor for those with mental health problems, and was advised that that although gradually returning to work was going to be quite difficult and complex, it could be done. It was important to be supported through this, not only in an emotional capacity, but with the administration that was needed to keep the Department for Work and Pensions up-to-date at all times. A common quote in all the department's literature is 'you must let us know if your circumstance change', which I did throughout, but I still came across difficulties as sometimes the evidence of my earnings failed to arrive by post or was not processed properly.

This caused me immense frustration, but somehow I kept telling myself that it would not be forever and that it would be worth it in the end. The Disability Employment Advisor supported me with applications and notified the benefit agencies as to my status, and I was also able to chat with her if I was feeling stressed. An opportunity arose to be a support worker for people with mental health problems who had been in a long-stay hospital environment. As I needed to stay under a set weekly earnings limit, I had to be very clear at interview stage about the number of hours that I could be employed. Fortunately, I was successful in my application and was absolutely delighted, as well as very nervous, but I knew that I needed to take things at my own pace and not jump in the deep end. I was able to work one shift a week and was surprised to settle into it well, but was under no illusion that doing this full-time would be a very different story. At times, though, whenever I saw full-time jobs in the paper I was very tempted to apply. Soon I was given a sessional position with another organization. It was a support worker role, helping people with mental health problems in the community and assisting them with their recovery and independence. There was scope for more variety and further learning.

By the end of 2006, I had completed three years with the Open University; secured a contract as a support worker working twenty-one hours a week; and went from attending the gym three times a week to running outside. In terms of finances, I had moved away from being on benefits, but fortunately there was a two-year period of protection, so that if I became unwell and unable to continue working at any time I wouldn't have to reapply for the benefits again. This gave me some security and eased some anxieties about moving on to the next stage in my recovery.

I had never felt more in control and happy than I had at this point – all the hard work had paid off and, although I continued with medication, I was realizing that a combined approach was vital in maintaining good mental health. This was not just about exercise and pacing: it was important for me to sleep well, eat well, stick to a routine and, if I was having a bad day, to reduce over-stimulation. My brain at times is unable to cope with over-stimulation so when I feel like this, it's been important for me to find a quiet place to relax (too much noise and mixed sounds make it worse), keep away from crowded areas, reduce contact and take part in yoga and meditation exercises. I have also been very fortunate to have my husband, who has been my best supporter, friend and companion, at my side at all times! By this time I had become a much better communicator of my difficulties, choosing to share them rather than keep them close by, and this too has been a great help.

By the end of 2007, I had completed four charity runs, including two 10 km runs, and was amazed at myself. The surprise was partly to do with the sheer enjoyment I gained from running as this was something that I never thought would happen. Running outside brought me a great sense of freedom and a chance to clear my head. I decided to enter a half-marathon in 2008, but unfortunately I had to pull out as I developed a chronic pain condition which has proved difficult to diagnose. However, it has become apparent that all the work in my recovery, which has spanned eight years, has not been for nothing as it has equipped me with the tools and skills to try and manage this pain as best as I can.

New opportunities have arisen in recent years and one of those was a new job. I realized quite early on that I was struggling to get around as a support worker in the community, as I was travelling on buses and getting very tired. I took my time to look for a more suitable job but found one with another mental health charity. My relatively new job could not be better and I feel very fortunate to be in the position I'm in. I've not been able to do any form of aerobic exercise since the beginning of 2008 because of my chronic pain and I am now using physical support services to maintain mobility and reduce pain and tiredness. Ironically I probably take more medication for my physical condition than I ever did for depression, but depression is a truly torturous condition and I'm so glad I'm not in that place.

While at times I still feel down, it is a very different feeling to that I endured for over fifteen years. Not only is it nowhere near as extreme and severe, but it is not long lasting and I still feel very much in control. I have maintained my interest in things and my hunger to keep learning. Time used to drag so slowly and I'd wish for the end of each day – now I wish I could slow time down as there are not enough hours in the day to fit everything in!

These days there are big differences in the support that people can access, and I have made sure that I keep a mental note to use these should the need arise.

I also thrive immensely on information technology, running my website, everything to do with the internet, portable gaming devices, computer hardware and software. It keeps my brain active, interested and hungry for more, and opens up new things for me to learn and do. I've learnt through all this that although depression is a very individual experience, you don't have to go through it alone. My mistake, for a long while, was not effectively using the support that has been around me. I couldn't involve my family, except my husband, in my journey so it was important to use other services. It helps to have family support, including when you need to apply pressure if you feel that a health professional is failing in their duty of care.

Another very big lesson is that mental health is seen

very differently to physical conditions. While this is changing, the stigma surrounding mental health was a big barrier for me in seeking help. What I was going through couldn't be seen, it was invisible, therefore I felt invisible. I had to put so much more effort and thought into seeking support and help because everything had to be described, but the invisibility of my internal distress meant that understanding and acknowledgement was hard to come by. With depression, it very much has to be said that those who've been through it or are going through it, including family, friends and carers, will be the most supportive people you will find to help you through your journey.

If you are close to someone you know or think has depression, be there for them. Let them talk if they need to, but also give them space. Encourage them to seek help and maybe go with them to appointments. Get information on the condition yourself as there are so many organizations that have literature and support for carers.

I am in a much better position now to go forward into the future knowing that I have the experience, knowledge and support to continue my journey. I'll be forty next year and I'll have been with my husband for twenty years. We balance our lives well between work and home life. We value spending quality time together and the sacrifices we've made by not having children and living in a small flat mean that we've kept things simple and uncomplicated.

There is hope. Depression is a treatable condition – it's just that for some it takes that bit longer to recover and finding things that help you through it is a very individual experience. Keep sight of how you felt before you were depressed and use the skills you already have to get yourself through it.

7

First-time mum

The thought of becoming pregnant and having a child was the scariest prospect I could ever have imagined in my life.

I had been with my fiancé for twelve years. We lived in a nice house with a car and a dog so you'd think the next step to have a child would have been an easy decision to make.

From the age of about twenty-five onwards friends and relatives would often ask when I was going to have children and say, 'It'll be your turn next.' Every time I heard this I'd have a heavy heart as, in all honesty, I could never see the time coming.

The reason behind my fear of becoming a parent was that my mother had suffered from post-natal depression and as a child I had seen the effect it had on her, although I hadn't fully understood it. I also worried that the chances of me suffering from post-natal depression were very high as I'd suffered from depression in the past. I also worried about what would happen I became unable to look after my child. My partner worked full-time and so I was worried that if I was unable to look after my child, he would have to stop working and this would cause terrible consequences in our life.

I have suffered with depression for many years, on and off. My lowest point was back in 2007 when I spent three months living with my parents as I was unable to eat, sleep or function very well day-to-day because of my depression. I was prescribed antidepressants and did eventually get better but this time in my life was very scary and continues to haunts me as I worry about feeling that low again. If I was to become depressed when I had a child, the repercussions would be more serious. I also worried about my child seeing me depressed as I had experienced that myself and I felt that it had a great effect on me in my adult life.

In the end I decided to bite the bullet and I finally became pregnant. At first I found it hard to allow myself to believe I was actually pregnant. In one sense I suppose I was in denial; I thought that if I didn't allow myself to become attached to my unborn child, it would affect me less if I then lost her. Throughout my pregnancy I worried I would miscarry and I always imagined the worst. The nine months seemed like an eternity. Unfortunately, I experienced some complications during my pregnancy and so had to be closely monitored at the hospital. However, I began to focus on my next appointment, which helped me to focus on time in a more constructive way. Looking back, I'm amazed at how well I got through the pregnancy despite my anxiety. I worried a lot of about the different bad things that might happen, but in the end I didn't experience any anxiety attacks during this period. I think I was very focused on not passing on any stress to my unborn child as I was determined that I didn't want anything to affect the baby.

I had always had a poor appetite and low weight before becoming pregnant, and I was worried I wouldn't eat enough to feed my unborn child, which in turn would hinder its development, and this would be my fault. I felt I would not have been able to live with this. Fortunately, both my appetite and weight improved during my pregnancy.

I felt a great sense of loss of control during my pregnancy. I'd read all the books and wanted to know all the ifs, buts and maybes, but I knew it was really just a case of having to let nature taking its course and waiting nine months. Unfortunately, I felt very let down by my consultant who wasn't able to reassure me enough and didn't have the answers I felt I needed. The complications during my pregnancy, coupled with my anxiety as a first-time mum, made it frustrating when I felt I was always getting textbook answers, rather than real-life answers. I knew that he didn't have a crystal ball and couldn't tell me how my pregnancy would turn out, but with his experience I thought that he could give me a better idea than he did.

Whenever I felt my baby moving inside me, it was an overwhelming feeling and, although I tried not to, I worried constantly when I hadn't felt her move for five minutes or so. My partner was very critical of my worrying and felt I had a negative attitude. I tried to explain to him that although he was obviously also going through the pregnancy with me and it was his baby too, it was different being a mother and actually feeling the baby growing inside you. You feel every movement the baby makes so it's very hard to simply switch off and forget about it.

When I had my scan and we were given the chance to find out the sex of the baby, my partner was very keen to find out. Beforehand he hadn't been too bothered but something changed that day and he decided he really wanted to know. When I'd had previous scans I could never really get my head around the fact that the pictures on the screen were images of the baby inside me. I would even say to the sonographer that the picture must have been of the last woman's baby. When we found out that our baby was a girl it scared me as I'd had a bad relationship with my mother when I was a child and I felt like history could repeat itself in some way. Knowing the sex also made the prospect of having a baby feel more real and harder to deny. However, one good thing was that I'd decided that there was no point in getting anxious about the birth before it happened because there was nothing I could do about it.

Arranging for my mum to be at the birth made me feel very relieved as she'd had three children of her own and I knew that if my anxiety became too much she'd under-stand how I felt. That in itself made me feel a whole lot better.

While I was pregnant I kept in contact with a midwife who helped ladies with mental health problems through-out their pregnancy. The support I got was invaluable. She was there on the other end of the phone and I could pop into the hospital to see her and have a chat when I needed to. I felt very safe in her presence and she made me feel more at ease with everything. I felt I could ask or tell her anything and she gave me the information I needed. Without this support, I worry that the anxiety would have been overwhelming.

At a birthing class I attended, the midwife explained that the anxiety hormone can hinder the progression of labour and so I made a mental note that to get through the labour I needed to try to not be anxious for both myself and my unborn child.

My waters broke two days before I gave birth. Looking back I can't believe how calm I was. I think I still had the thoughts in my mind of what the midwife had said about anxiety – I went a little dizzy in the hospital when the midwife confirmed this, but then I think any woman would!

The whole labour and birth seems pretty surreal to me now. When I watch ladies on TV giving birth, it often seems to be very emotional but it wasn't like that for me. Towards the end of my labour things became quite frantic as my baby became distressed. When I gave birth to her they handed her over to me only for a short time before whisking her to the special care baby unit, where she was monitored as a precautionary measure. I was quickly taken to theatre, which made me feel more anxious than the whole birth.

When I finally got to see my daughter again, ten hours later, I was very tired and the enormity of the fact she was mine still hadn't really sunk in. She came back up to the ward with me and now the responsibility of caring for her became mine.

I personally find the most overwhelming part of caring for my daughter is the sense of responsibility. This tiny little person relies on you every second of every day and you worry if every decision you make is the right one. I felt constantly guilty about whether what I was doing was right or wrong.

For many months following the birth, I felt very detached from my daughter. I did everything in my power to care for her well and did everything I could so that she would not suffer in any way. However I still felt that I could not allow myself to love her as I worried that if I became attached to her something bad may happen. I felt like someone was going to knock at the door and say, 'Thanks for looking after our baby – we'll have her back now.' I knew deep down that this wasn't going to happen but, nonetheless, this is what I felt.

I felt very anxious after giving birth to my daughter but I hid it well as I'd read that babies can pick up on things like that. I don't know how I managed it because on the one hand I felt like I was out of my depth looking after my daughter, while on the other hand I would sometimes worry that I was going over the top in the way I cared for her. If I could have wrapped her up in cotton wool and then put her in a bubble I would have!

I was very worried in the early months that people would think I was not capable of looking after my daughter, but people often commented on how well I was doing, although I didn't always believe them when they complimented me – I thought they were just saying it to try and make me feel better about myself. Luckily, my daughter was a very content baby from the start and once she fell into a good routine she was amazing. People have told me this is down to me but I still find it hard to believe – I felt this was my daughter's doing.

In the back of my mind I constantly worried about getting post-natal depression: I felt like it was a time bomb waiting to go off. I'd ask myself questions such as how soon it was going to happen. A little while after having my daughter, my old thoughts and feelings of depression began to creep back; my appetite dwindled; my sleep pattern was erratic anyway; and I felt a little down as my main focus in life before having my daughter had been work. Some people feel that having a child is what they were put on this earth to do, but that wasn't how I felt – I loved my job. The severity of my depressed thoughts and feelings returned to what they were prior to my pregnancy. I didn't feel they were a cause for concern in the sense that I had support around me from professional bodies.

Before I had become pregnant one of my biggest fears had been of not having someone professional to talk to when I was feeling bad – I'd had times when I'd felt depressed and gone to see my GP, only to be put on a waiting list to see a specialist and sent away with antidepressants. However, after my daughter was born, I received much better support and was even offered the chance to try a new therapy. It was a group therapy, which I'd never experienced before. The Compassion Focused Therapy made me think about things in a whole different way. I am a very analytical person and have been for as long as I can remember. I always try to understand my thoughts and feelings, and the Compassion Focused Therapy helped me do this a little better. It gave me the principles and techniques to allow me to approach the difficulties I encounter on a daily basis in a different way. It made me realize that all my feelings and emotions, no matter how dark, are transitory – they come and they go. Like all therapy I have received in the past, it has given me invaluable knowledge into the makeup of my being, which has given me great strength and determination to lead a better life in bringing up my daughter. The new therapy helped me come to terms with some of my unanswered questions.

I also received great comfort from meeting likeminded people in a non-judgemental environment where we could freely express our deepest, darkest thoughts. I knew other people were going through the same things as me but to be together in a room once a week made all the difference. However painful it felt to express what I was feeling and to hear other people's stories, I really enjoyed the closeness I shared with these people as they were the only people I could trust with my thoughts and feelings. I felt a great understanding of myself and the others in the group and wished that we didn't have to battle with our anxieties and depression on a day-to-day basis. I felt a great sadness when the sessions came to an end and I think I also found leaving my daughter for a few hours each week gave me some independence back, as up to that point I cared for her most days in the week while my partner was at work. However, it hadn't been easy to hand the reins over to someone else to care for her – I felt guilty that someone else was caring for her, not me.

My decision to go back to work was a hard one. I felt very selfish and that I was putting my own needs before those of my daughter. In the long run I knew that if I didn't put my needs first in this situation it would inevitably affect my daughter. My twelve-month maternity leave would have taken me up to January. At first my decision was to take the full twelve-month entitlement but

I knew that the onset of the winter months would increase my depression and I would feel better if I was working. So, after much consideration, I decided to go back to work after nine months. This was the best decision I made.

Before having my daughter I had really enjoyed my job with a passion: it gave me great focus in my life. Going back to work put my life into a good routine and my daughter benefited from this greatly too. I decided to place her with a child-minder and sought out someone who had older children of her own. I felt very out of control again when I handed over care of my daughter to someone else and I worried that she wouldn't care for her in exactly the way I wanted. However, my fears were unfounded as my child-minder was very patient with me and listened to what I wanted from her. She was very considerate of my fears and feelings and I could not have asked for any more from her. She has been a true blessing to me and has given me great encouragement, guidance and compassion in my struggle with being a first-time mum. I soon realized that my child-minder was doing an amazing job – I could see my daughter's development on a daily basis, and how happy and content she was.

Gradually I realized my daughter was chipping away at the walls around my heart. On some days when I was feeling down she would say a word or a tooth would come through and it seemed to put my feelings into perspective and give me a warm glow in my heart. I definitely feel like I have a purpose in life now. Previously I felt like my smile didn't always reach my eyes, but these days my cheeks hurt sometimes with all the smiles and laughter! Knowing what I know now, I wish I'd have made the decision to have a baby five years or so earlier. I still find it very surreal that I went through it all but came out the other end and survived.

8

The key to the invisible prison

I would like to dedicate this to my Granddad. He was not given the support and help needed to fight depression and it took his life, like it has taken the lives of so many. Yet because of him I feel I can fight depression and control my life – all of us sufferers can. If you are scared, then don't be, as there is support and treatment that can work and there is a way out. I hope my story can help you.

Ever since I could remember I was depressed. Of course, when I was a child I had no idea what was wrong with me. All I knew was that I always had suicidal thoughts, thinking I would be better off dead and, worst of all, not knowing why I felt this way.

For years I thought I was ungrateful, self-indulgent and spoilt – after all, I wasn't starving in Africa – and then I started to think that maybe I was mad in some way and that perhaps my brain had some kind of weird defect. As I got older and into my teens I thought I was weak, that I couldn't handle life, and I was scared that if people found out that I felt this way they would laugh at me and think I was stupid and feeble-minded. Some days I had no control on my emotions: I would wake up with a longing to die, or I would look in the mirror and hate myself or simply just want to cry. At the time my family life wasn't great. My older sister was very cruel and would often play on my fears, telling me that I was ugly and stupid, and bullying me. My parents would join in with the name-calling. Of course, this happens all the time in families but when you're depressed you believe what people tell you because that's how you feel yourself. It chips your confidence and feeds your self-doubt.

You end up suffering in silence, for fear of people's reactions. You start to believe that you are ungrateful and that you should just pull yourself together. In my teenage years I made many attempts to take my life; sometimes it was just a cry for help, other times I wanted to die. The last time I took an overdose was when I was twenty-one, thirteen years ago. I haven't done it since, but I have thought about it often. After all, that's a symptom of depression, but I have tried my hardest not to act on these thoughts anymore and have succeeded. If these types of thoughts continue it means that your depression is strong and you need to ask for help. Of course, it's easy for me to say this now. I was diagnosed with clinical depression when I was twenty-six and only now, after further episodes of illness, do I know that I suffer from both chronic depression and generalized anxiety disorder (GAD).

Now I know that other people suffer from depression too – successful people, famous people and even clever people! The relief I found from this is amazing: I have a diagnosis, there are other people like me, it's common and I have a treatment plan – and it is helping. I can finally share my feelings with other people, including friends, family and colleagues. It's as if someone has given me a key to break out of an invisible prison.

My virtual prison sentence lasted a long time – from about the age of four onwards. Some years were quite good, with only short episodes of depression of a few weeks or months, whilst during other years it felt constant.

I was twenty-five when I had my first recognized breakdown (I may well have had 'official' breakdowns at other times, but I wasn't told). I had been very depressed for months – I became very withdrawn, didn't socialize as much and lost a lot of weight. I was always a very sociable person so my friends did notice a difference in me, plus they all kept going on at me about how skinny I was. Work was very stressful but I was still able to be efficient and get things done. I had a few issues with family to deal with so I decided to get some counselling. This didn't turn out as well as I had hoped. I didn't get the right counsellor and found the whole process very difficult. In the end, I have come to believe that it was the counselling which lead to my breakdown, but in some ways I do see that this was a positive thing because I would never have been diagnosed otherwise. I would strongly advocate that, if you do go through counselling, find someone you feel comfortable with and get as much information as possible about the process. I doubt very much that I will ever return to the kind of counselling I had at the time – it really wasn't right for me – but I know that for others it really does work.

The breakdown itself was a long time coming. I had been depressed for a very long time. It felt like I had lost the use of my legs – some days, no matter how much I tried, I just couldn't walk and on other days I felt like I was crawling through life. I tried to treat the depression myself. As well as the counselling, I started doing regular exercise and I even tried to change my diet, all of which was good but I needed more than that to get better. I had been 'crawling' for some time when a friend came over to see me; she said that she was worried about me, about my weight loss and my behaviour, and she suggested that I was depressed. I remember her talking to me and all I could do was cry. It was uncontrollable and I was rocking my body to try and stop myself but I just couldn't. I was exhausted and I knew then that I had to get help.

I went to my GP and told her the truth about how I felt, and she diagnosed me with clinical depression. I was just given a prescription for antidepressants and returned to work. I thought that I would start to feel better and that life would continue as normal, but of course it doesn't work that way – it's not as easy as that. The first drug treatment didn't seem to suit me and the side-effects were too strong. The next set of drugs were OK but I developed an allergy to them. The third drug was better: it worked and the side-effects were minimal. I took two weeks off work, went home to my parent's house and started to recover.

I told my sister about my diagnosis first, over the phone, and then told my mum face to face. Luckily she was very supportive and, being a psychiatric nurse, was able to at least understand the condition and not get scared. My dad didn't want to believe I had depression and didn't really acknowledge it. This was because there was depression on his side of the family; my paternal grandfather suffered with depression and sadly took his life when he was sixty-four, dying from an overdose. In those days when someone committed suicide it was very shameful and people didn't talk about it. I only recently found out about it and I was devastated to know that he had no help – it didn't have to be that way. In some way this has made me work harder at getting better. My dad and some of his other siblings also suffered from depression and I guess they have always been scared of the same fate as their father, and have never wanted to admit it to themselves.

I was prescribed a SNRI which worked really well and gave me my life back. In the two weeks off I mainly gave into the depression for a few days. I would just sleep and do nothing, which I found was really what I needed. After my time off I went back to work and also managed to complete the purchase of a flat. I felt that I had achieved a lot given my state of mind and that perhaps this would be the end of my depression. I lost a few friends in the process of my breakdown and initial recovery but the ones that did support me were fantastic and I became closer to my parents. In hindsight, though, I probably needed more time off. I became a bit too obsessed with keeping myself busy and organized, and I think that this was fed by general anxiety disorder. I worried far too much if things didn't get done for whatever reason. At this point, I wasn't aware that general anxiety disorder actually existed: I just thought I was someone who worried a lot and I tried to deal with it my own way. After about a year of being on antidepressants I decided that I didn't need them anymore and wanted to take control over my life. I took it upon myself to initially reduce my dose, and then one day I stopped taking them. The side-effects of coming off them were not great and it was a while before I felt myself again. I coped fine for a few years – my anxiety wasn't too bad and I felt much better, so I was convinced that the depression was over. Then, aged twenty-nine, the depression started again.

At first it was mild. I guess that I ignored it and helped to mask it by going out, drinking excessively and just having fun. But along with the hangovers, there was the feeling of depression – I used to just put it down to having 'booze blues'. Deep down I knew it was back, but I just carried on drinking to hide it and I even took recreational drugs to get rid of the feeling. I just didn't want to go back on the antidepressants – I thought that would be a step backwards and I had come so far without them. But, worst of all, it would mean the depression was back and I guess I wasn't ready to confront it. The depression was like having this rain cloud over me. I used everything in my power to take cover from the constant rain by drinking and taking drugs but it was here to stay.

I then decided to change my lifestyle. I stopped taking drugs and cut down on my alcohol intake, and I decided to learn how to drive in an attempt to give myself a challenge and to give my mind something else to think about. I kept my evenings busy with constructive things, like cooking and cleaning, and I tried hard not to have to think. It worked some days but other days it was really difficult and I just couldn't get out of bed. Because I had become so good at trying to ignore my depression it came out in other ways. I started getting chronic back pain, my stress levels were very high all the time and panic attacks became part of my everyday life.

What I now realize was that this was part of my generalized anxiety disorder (GAD), and whilst I had previously treated the depression I had done nothing for my GAD. Thinking back now I think I had GAD from a young age and it may well have started because of my childhood, which was difficult and often traumatic. It could also be genetic because I can see it in my dad, but it could have been the result of a number of things. What matters is that I got my diagnosis and sought treatment. Finding out about the symptoms was a real revelation as all this time I just thought they were part of my personality – a part I didn't like. Now I can see that they don't have to be and the cognitive behavioural therapy (CBT) I was to start imminently helped me to understand this.

My depression was back but I knew I had to do something about it before it was too late. It was bad. I was back in that invisible prison again. I felt I was close to another breakdown and I knew I had to take action. At first I was really scared of doing it, but I knew that I couldn't live like this anymore and I knew that it could get better. I just had to take control but I needed help. I was thirty-two when I finally plucked up the courage to go to my GP again.

My GP was very good as she initially gave me lots of information about both depression and GAD, and the treatments involved which included CBT. I was also asked to do a questionnaire so that she could assess me properly, which was useful for me because it put things in perspective. I could see how depressed I was and that I really did need help.

I was then given a week to decide whether or not I wanted to go ahead with the treatment and she told me to talk to friends and family to get support, and also to tell my boss. I was worried about doing that all again but thankfully everyone was very supportive. I decided to go back on the antidepressants – after all, if I had been diagnosed with diabetes I wouldn't think twice about taking insulin, and it wasn't a step back: it was a step forward. Some people only have depression for a certain period of time but for me it was part of my life, it was who I was and for the first time I accepted that.

I was initially very scared of the CBT treatment. I was worried about how it would affect me and what I would find out. However, the first session was much better than I thought. It was over the phone and my therapist talked me through the process. We went through the questionnaire I had filled out and then arranged an appointment. The first face-to-face meeting was mainly informative; we talked about what I felt I needed to do and how to go about the process. I didn't feel bad or weak or scared anymore: my life would begin to start again. I started a new job and was feeling on top of everything. After a few sessions I thought that I really didn't need the therapy anymore, but I was wrong.

In fact, I found the new job was very stressful and in my fragile state it was just too much. I resigned and decided that I would take a break. This time I would put my mental health first. I felt good about doing it and in the first week of being off work I realized how much I needed the time out. I was exhausted. I had lost weight and was not in a good place.

So, I decided to continue with the antidepressants and returned to see my therapist once a week. I could soon see the changes. Now my anxiety disorder is much better than it has ever been and the depression is much better too. The CBT has really changed my life and given me real hope of getting better and staying that way. I'm still seeing my therapist and I'm given tasks and ways in which to change my behaviour.

I've also been on workshops aimed at improving my sleep and stress-levels. The workshops have been really beneficial. I have met other people in the same situation and it is just great to be able to talk to others who have been going through the same things as me. There are loads of people in my situation and we are all trying hard to help ourselves.

I would be lying if I said I didn't have any bad days because they are still there, but I can cope with them much better now and I am able to feel more in control. The CBT is hard and does make me anxious sometimes because of the fear that it will change me as a person. Actually, it has changed me but I prefer the person I am now. Some days I wake up without worry and I feel happy, even when things aren't going so well in my life. Somehow, with the help of the therapy and the medication, it's all OK.

I know I will always have depression and anxiety issues. I have accepted this now but the CBT has helped me understand them – it has given me tools to deal with them and I know that I can move forward. Also, if I do get ill I can identify the warning signs and do something before things get worse. I never in my wildest dreams thought I would be in a position to say that, and yet here I am. I still have a lot more hard work to do but I'm excited about moving forward and getting there. I'm not terrified of getting ill anymore and can see the light in the tunnel. I finally broke free from my invisible prison and I'm getting the right kind of rehabilitation. It took a long time to get here but I'm here now and I intend on staying here! I would urge anyone in the same position to try and do the same. I know it's hard and seems hopeless but it doesn't have to be that way.

Support groups, charities and other resources for those suffering from depression

Support groups and charities

MIND (The National Association for Mental Health)
15–19 Broadway
Stratford
London E15 4BQ
Tel: 0845 766 0163
Email: contact@mind.org.uk
Website: www.mind.org.uk

MDF (The Bipolar Organisation)
Castle Works
21 St George's Road
London SE1 6ES
Tel: 020 7793 2600
Email: mdf@mdf.org.uk
Website: www.mdf.org.uk

Depression Alliance
20 Great Dover Street
London SE1 4LX
Tel: 0845 1232320
Website: www.depressionalliance.org
Email: information@depressionalliance.org

Association for Postnatal Illness
145 Dawes Road
Fulham
London
SW6 7EB
Tel: 020 7386 0868
Website: http://apni.org

SANE
First Floor
Cityside House
40 Adler Street
London E1 1EE
Tel: 020 7375 1002
Email: info@sane.org.uk
Website: www.sane.org.uk

Samaritans
PO Box 9090
Stirling FK8 2SA
Tel: 08457 909090
Email: jo@samaritans.org
Website: www.samaritans.org

British Association for Behavioural and Cognitive Psychotherapies
Imperial House
Hornby Street
Bury BL9 5BN
Tel: 0161 705 4304
Email: babcp@babcp.com
Website: www.babcp.com

Books

Overcoming Depression by Paul Gilbert, Robinson, 2009
The Worry Cure by Robert Leahy, Piatkus Books, 2006
Manage Your Mood by David Veale and Rob Willson, Robinson, 2008
Overcoming Depression: A Five Areas Approach by Chris Williams, Arnold, 2001
The Mindful Way through Depression by Mark Williams, John Teasdale, Zindel Segal and Jon Kabat-Zinn, Guilford Press, 2007
Meditation for Beginners by J. Kornfield, Bantam Books, 2004
The Compassionate Mind by Paul Gilbert, Constable, 2009
Coming to Our Senses: Healing Ourselves and the World through Mindfulness by Jon Kabat-Zinn, Piatkus, 2005

Websites

Beyondblue, www.beyondblue.org.au
Living Life to the Full, www.livinglifetothefull.com

Index

Order now and save money

Quantity	Title	RRP	Offer Price	Total
	An Introduction to Coping with Anxiety (pack of 10)	£29.99	£10	
	An Introduction to Coping with Depression (pack of 10)	£29.99	£10	
	An Introduction to Coping with Grief (pack of 10)	£29.99	£10	
	An Introduction to Coping with Health Anxiety (pack of 10)	£29.99	£10	
	An Introduction to Coping with Obsessive Compulsive Disorder (pack of 10)	£29.99	£10	
	An Introduction to Coping with Panic (pack of 10)	£29.99	£10	
	An Introduction to Coping with Phobias (pack of 10)	£29.99	£10	
	An Introduction to Coping with Post-Traumatic Stress (pack of 10)	£29.99	£10	
	An Introduction to Coping with Stress (pack of 10)	£29.99	£10	
	Overcoming Anger and Irritability	£9.99	£7.99	
	Overcoming Anorexia Nervosa	£9.99	£7.99	
	Overcoming Anxiety	£9,99	£7.99	
	Overcoming Anxiety Self-Help Course (3 parts)	£21	£18	
	Overcoming Bulimia Nervosa and Binge-Eating	£9.99	£7.99	
	Overcoming Bulimia and Binge-Eating Self-Help Course (3 parts)	£21	£18	
	Overcoming Childhood Trauma	£9.99	£7.99	
	Overcoming Chronic Fatigue	£9.99	£7.99	
	Overcoming Chronic Pain	£9.99	£7.99	
	Overcoming Compulsive Gambling	£9.99	£7.99	
	Overcoming Depression	£9.99	£7.99	
	Overcoming Insomnia and Sleeping Problems	£9.99	£7.99	
	Overcoming Low Self-Esteem	£9.99	£7.99	
	Overcoming Low Self-Esteem Self-Help Course (3 parts)	£21	£18	
	Overcoming Mood Swings	£9.99	£7.99	
	Overcoming Obsessive Compulsive Disorder	£9.99	£7.99	
	Overcoming Panic	£9.99	£7.99	
	Overcoming Panic and Agoraphobia Self-Help Course (3 parts)	£21	£18	
	Overcoming Paranoid and Suspicious Thoughts	£9.99	£7.99	
	Overcoming Problem Drinking	£9.99	£7.99	
	Overcoming Relationship Problems	£9.99	£7.99	

Order now and save money

		£9.99	**£7.99**	
	Over coming Sexual Problems	£9.99	**£7.99**	
	Overcoming Social Anxiety and Shyness	£9.99	**£7.99**	
	Overcoming Social Anxiety and Shyness Self-Help Course (3 parts)	£21	**£18**	
	Overcoming Traumatic Stress	£9.9 9	**£7.99**	
	Overcoming Weight Problems	£9.99	**£7.99**	
	Overcoming Your Child's Fears and Worries	£9.99	**£7.99**	
	Overcoming Your Smoking Habit	£9.99	**£7.99**	
	P&P		**FREE**	
			Grand TOTAL	

Name: _____

Address: _____

_____ Postcode: _____

Daytime Tel. No.: _____ Email: _____

How to pay:

1 **By telephone:** call the TBS order line on **01206 255 800** and quote **BEAT.** Phone lines are open between Monday-Friday, 8.30am-5.30pm.

2 **By** post: send a cheque for the full amount payable to TBS Ltd. and send form to:
Freepost RLUL-SJGC-SGKJ, Cash Sales/Direct Mail Dept., The Book Service, Colchester Road, Frating, Colchester C07 7DW.

Is/are the book(s) intended for personal use ☐ or professional use ☐?
Please note this information will not be passed on to third parties.

Constable & Robinson Ltd (directly or via its agents) may mail or phone you about promotions or products. Tick box if you do not want these from us ☐ or our subsidiaries ☐.

Overcoming Depression

A self-help guide using Cognitive Behavioral Techniques, fully revised third edition

'Highly recommended' *Sunday Times*

If you suffer from depression you are far from alone. Depression is very common, affecting over 300 million people around the world. Written by Professor Paul Gilbert, internationally recognized for his work on depression, this highly acclaimed self-help book has been of benefit to thousands of people including sufferers, their friends and families, and those working in the medical profession.

This fully revised third edition has been extensively updated and rewritten to reflect over ten years of new research on understanding and treating depression, particularly the importance of developing compassionate ways of thinking, behaving and feeling. It contains helpful case studies and new, easy-to-follow, step-by-step suggestions and exercises to help you understand your depression and lift your mood.

978-1-84901-066-5
£12.99

Visit www.constablerobinson.com for more information

Taking Control of OCD

Inspirational Stories of Hope and Recovery

'Reading this book is one of the best ways to understand the devastating impact that OCD has and how, with support and dedication, it can be overcome.' *OCD Action*

Obsessive Compulsive Disorder (OCD) can come in a variety of guises ranging from obsessive hand-washing and checking of electrical appliances, to hoarding or experiencing disturbing and intrusive thoughts of a sexual or even murderous nature. The symptoms of this disorder are often extremely upsetting for the sufferer and for those around them, and often misunderstood.

This collection of real-life accounts of coping with, and overcoming OCD, will provide inspiration to anyone going through similar experiences and those who care for them. Each story, especially selected by world-renowned experts on OCD, David Veale and Rob Willson, has been written by someone with first-hand experience of the illness and offers a unique understanding of the illness, useful insights into what helps and, most importantly, inspiration to those trying to beat this difficult condition.

978-1-84901-401-4
£9.99

Visit www.constablerobinson.com for more information

How to Beat your Fears & Worries

How to Stop Worrying and Start Living

We all have fears and we all worry from time to time, but if this starts
to take over and affect your quality of life, it's time for action.
Cognitive Behavioral Therapy (CBT), on which this self-help book is based,
is a proven, effective treatment for anxiety. It helps you to combat
anxious thoughts and to change the behaviours that keep your anxiety going,
so that you can put fear back in its place and lead a happier,
more fulfilling life.

978-1-84901-399-4
£7.99

Visit www.constablerobinson.com for more information